Practical Monitoring
Effective Strategies for the Real World

Mike Julian

Beijing · Boston · Farnham · Sebastopol · Tokyo

Practical Monitoring

by Mike Julian

Copyright © 2018 Mike Julian. All rights reserved.

Published by O'Reilly Media, Inc., 1005 Gravenstein Highway North, Sebastopol, CA 95472.

O'Reilly books may be purchased for educational, business, or sales promotional use. Online editions are also available for most titles (*http://oreilly.com/safari*). For more information, contact our corporate/institutional sales department: 800-998-9938 or *corporate@oreilly.com*.

Editors: Virginia Wilson and Nikki McDonald	**Indexer:** Wendy Catalano
Production Editor: Justin Billing	**Interior Designer:** David Futato
Copyeditor: Dwight Ramsey	**Cover Designer:** Karen Montgomery
Proofreader: Amanda Kersey	**Illustrator:** Rebecca Demarest

November 2017:   First Edition

Revision History for the First Edition
2017-10-26:   First Release
2017-11-27:   Second Release

See *http://oreil.ly/2y3s5AB* for release details.

978-1-491-95735-6

[LSI]

Table of Contents

Part I.   Monitoring Principles

Part II.   Monitoring Tactics

To Leonard, for sparking my curiosity in tech at a young age.

*To my parents, for stoking that curiosity and putting up with
my constant all-nighters in front of the computer.*

*To Donna and Justine, for taking a huge chance and
giving me my first job (in tech, even!).*

*To Mrs. Sedor, who showed me the joy of literature,
both in understanding it and creating it.*

To all my dear friends, without whom life wouldn't be nearly as enjoyable.

Preface

The monitoring landscape of today is vastly different than it was only a few years ago, and even more so than it was 10 years ago. With the widespread popularity of cloud infrastructure came new problems for monitoring, as well as creating new ways to solve old problems.

The rise in popularity of microservices has especially stretched how we think about monitoring. Since there is no longer a monolithic app server, how do we monitor interactions between the dozens, or even hundreds, of small app servers that communicate constantly? A common pattern in microservice architecture is that a server may exist for only hours or even minutes, which has wreaked havoc on the age-old tactics and monitoring tools we once relied on.

Of course, while some things change, some things stay the same. We still worry about web server performance. We still have concerns over root volumes unexpectedly running out of space. Database server performance still keeps many of us awake at night. While some of the problems we have today are similar to (or the same as) the problems we had 10 years ago, the tools and methodologies available to us are much improved. It is my goal to teach you the advances we've made and how to leverage them for your purposes.

I believe it is helpful to bear in mind throughout this book what the purpose and goals of monitoring are. To that end, allow me to pass along a definition of *monitoring*. The best definition I've heard comes from Greg Poirier, proposed at the Monitorama 2016 conference (*https://vimeo.com/173610062*):

> Monitoring is the action of observing and checking the behavior and outputs of a system and its components over time.

This definition is broad, but rightly so: there's a lot under the monitoring umbrella, and we'll be covering it all: metrics, logging, alerting, on-call, incident management, postmortems, statistics, and much, much more.

Who Should Read This Book

If you deal with monitoring, this is the book for you. More specifically, this book is geared toward those seeking a foundational understanding of monitoring. It's suitable for junior staff as well as nontechnical staff looking to beef up their knowledge on monitoring.

If you already have a great grasp on monitoring, this probably is not the book for you. There are no deep dives into specific tools or discussions about monitoring at Google-scale. Instead, you will find practical, real-world examples and immediately actionable advice geared to those new to the world of monitoring.

Those looking for the next hot monitoring tool to implement will be disappointed. As I will discuss later in this book, there's no magic bullet for solving your monitoring challenges. As such, this book is tool-agnostic, though I certainly will mention specific tools from time to time as examples of what to do or not to do. Likewise, if you want to go deeper into a particular stack of tools, this book will not help.

A minimum level of technical knowledge is assumed for this book. I assume you know the basics of running servers and writing code. My examples all reference Linux, though the topics are still generically applicable for Windows administrators as well.

Why I Wrote This Book

Throughout my career, I've found myself as the unwitting champion for better monitoring. As we all know, the one who points out the problem signs up to fix it, which resulted in my doing more monitoring implementations than I can recall. Over time, I've noticed many people have the same questions about monitoring, sometimes phrased in different ways.

- My monitoring sucks. What should I do about it?
- My monitoring is OK, but I know I can do better. What should I be thinking about?
- My monitoring is noisy and no one trusts it. How can I permanently fix it?
- What stuff is the most important to monitor? Where do I even start?

These are all complex questions with complex answers. There's no single correct answer, but there are some great guiding principles that will get you where you want to go. This book will walk through these principles with plenty of examples.

This book is not the final word on monitoring, nor is it meant to be. This is the book I wish had existed when I first started getting serious about improving monitoring. There are plenty of great books that go deep on specific topics that I only touch on, so if you find yourself wanting to go there, I encourage it! I view this book as preparing for you a foundational skill level in the monitoring domain.

A Word on Monitoring Today

Monitoring is a quickly evolving topic. To make things more challenging, monitoring is a topic that will never reach a state of true maturity: every time we get close, our entire world changes. In the late '90s and early '00s, Nagios was king, and we were all pretty satisfied with it. Before long, we needed to start automating infrastructure due to the growing size of it all. People began doing interesting things with scaling it (e.g., Gearman, instant failover with custom heartbeats and DRBD) and managing the configuration (e.g., external datasources, custom UIs, and MySQL-backed configuration storage), completely stretching Nagios to its limits and revealing that our ways of thinking about monitoring were beginning to show their age. This has been repeated a few times since then, of course: cloud computing, containers, microservices.

While this constant change may frustrate some, it excites others. Take heart, though: the principles I will talk about are timeless.

Navigating This Book

The book is divided into two parts. Chapters 1 through 4 discuss principles of monitoring: anti-patterns to watch out for and new ways to think about monitoring. Chapters 5 through 11 are about monitoring tactics: what to monitor, why to do it, and how.

Online Resources

I have a companion website for this book at *https://www.practicalmonitoring.com*, which will contain additional resources and errata.

Conventions Used in This Book

The following typographical conventions are used in this book:

Italic
: Indicates new terms, URLs, email addresses, filenames, and file extensions.

`Constant width`
: Used for program listings, as well as within paragraphs to refer to program elements such as variable or function names, databases, data types, environment variables, statements, and keywords.

Constant width bold

> Shows commands or other text that should be typed literally by the user.

Constant width italic

> Shows text that should be replaced with user-supplied values or by values determined by context.

 This icon signifies a tip, suggestion, or general note.

 This element signifies a general note.

 This icon indicates a warning or caution.

Using Code Examples

This book is here to help you get your job done. In general, if example code is offered with this book, you may use it in your programs and documentation. You do not need to contact us for permission unless you're reproducing a significant portion of the code. For example, writing a program that uses several chunks of code from this book does not require permission. Selling or distributing a CD-ROM of examples from O'Reilly books does require permission. Answering a question by citing this book and quoting example code does not require permission. Incorporating a significant amount of example code from this book into your product's documentation does require permission.

We appreciate, but do not require, attribution. An attribution usually includes the title, author, publisher, and ISBN. For example: "*Practical Monitoring* by Mike Julian (O'Reilly). Copyright 2018, Mike Julian, 978-1-491-95735-6."

If you feel your use of code examples falls outside fair use or the permission given above, feel free to contact us at *permissions@oreilly.com*.

O'Reilly Safari

 *Safari* (formerly Safari Books Online) is a membership-based training and reference platform for enterprise, government, educators, and individuals.

Members have access to thousands of books, training videos, Learning Paths, interactive tutorials, and curated playlists from over 250 publishers, including O'Reilly Media, Harvard Business Review, Prentice Hall Professional, Addison-Wesley Professional, Microsoft Press, Sams, Que, Peachpit Press, Adobe, Focal Press, Cisco Press, John Wiley & Sons, Syngress, Morgan Kaufmann, IBM Redbooks, Packt, Adobe Press, FT Press, Apress, Manning, New Riders, McGraw-Hill, Jones & Bartlett, and Course Technology, among others.

For more information, please visit *http://oreilly.com/safari*.

How to Contact Us

Please address comments and questions concerning this book to the publisher:

O'Reilly Media, Inc.
1005 Gravenstein Highway North
Sebastopol, CA 95472
800-998-9938 (in the United States or Canada)
707-829-0515 (international or local)
707-829-0104 (fax)

We have a web page for this book, where we list errata, examples, and any additional information. You can access this page at *http://shop.oreilly.com/product/0636920050773.do*.

To comment or ask technical questions about this book, send email to *bookquestions@oreilly.com*.

For more information about our books, courses, conferences, and news, see our website at *http://www.oreilly.com*.

Find us on Facebook: *http://facebook.com/oreilly*

Follow us on Twitter: *http://twitter.com/oreillymedia*

Watch us on YouTube: *http://www.youtube.com/oreillymedia*

Acknowledgments

This book wouldn't be here without the help, advice, and support of many.

Many thanks to my technical reviewers, whose feedback made this a much better book than I ever thought it could be: Jess Males, John Wynkoop, Aaron Sachs, Heinrich Hartmann, and Tammy Butow. Thanks to Jason Dixon and Elijah Wright, who reviewed and gave feedback on the first outline of what would become this book and encouraged me to write it.

A huge thank you to my editors at O'Reilly: Brian Anderson, Virginia Wilson, and Angela Rufino. I must have driven you nuts with the many missed deadlines, so thank you for your patience and guidance. As a first-time author, your help was invaluable.

My writing progress seems to be positively correlated with my coffee consumption, leading me to have written the bulk of this book in coffee shops—often while traveling. Therefore, I would like to extend a special thanks to my dealers—er, baristas:

- Old City Java, Knoxville, TN
- Wild Love Bake House, Knoxville, TN
- Workshop Cafe, San Francisco, CA
- Hubsy, Paris, France
- OR Espresso Bar, Brussels, Belgium

If you ever find yourself in the neighborhood, I recommend stopping in for a great cup of coffee.

Many of the lessons I set out to teach in this book are not new—in fact, some are decades old in concept. Thusly, I cannot take all of the credit, for I've reworded and presented in new ways the thoughts and ideas of those who have come before me. That is to say, there is very little new in the world, and ideas in tech have a way of recycling themselves.

Monitoring Principles

Part I of *Practical Monitoring* will explore the guiding principles of monitoring. We'll be discussing anti-patterns, design patterns, alerting, and more. Part I will set the foundation for your monitoring journey.

## CHAPTER 1

Monitoring Anti-Patterns

Before we can start off on our journey to great monitoring, we have to identify and correct some bad habits you may have adopted or observed in your environment.

As with many habits, they start off well-meaning. After years of inadequate tools, the realities of keeping legacy applications running, and a general lack of knowledge about modern practices, these bad habits become "the way it's always been done" and are often taken with people when they leave one job for another. On the surface, they don't look that harmful. But rest assured—they are ultimately detrimental to a solid monitoring platform. For this reason, we'll refer to them as *anti-patterns*.

> An anti-pattern is something that looks like a good idea, but which backfires badly when applied.
>
> —Jim Coplien

These anti-patterns can often be difficult to fix for various reasons: entrenched practices and culture, legacy infrastructure, or just plain old FUD (fear, uncertainty, and doubt). We'll work through all of those, too, of course.

Anti-Pattern #1: Tool Obsession

There's a great quote from Richard Bejtlich in his book *The Practice of Network Security Monitoring* (No Starch Press, 2013) that underscores the problem with an excessive focus on tools over capabilities:

> Too many security organizations put tools before operations. They think "we need to buy a log management system" or "I will assign one analyst to antivirus duty, one to data leakage protection duty." And so on. A tool-driven team will not be effective as a mission-driven team. When the mission is defined by running software, analysts become captive to the features and limitations of their tools. Analysts who think in terms of what they need in order to accomplish their mission will seek tools to meet

those needs, and keep looking if their requirements aren't met. Sometimes they even decide to build their own tools.

—Richard Bejtlich

Many monitoring efforts start out the same way. "We need better monitoring!" someone says. Someone else blames the current monitoring toolset for the troubles they're experiencing and suggests evaluating new ones. Fast-forward six months and the cycle repeats itself.

If you learn nothing else from this book, remember this: there are no silver bullets.

Anything worth solving takes a bit of effort, and monitoring a complex system is certainly no exception. Relatedly, there is no such thing as the single-pane-of-glass tool that will suddenly provide you with perfect visibility into your network, servers, and applications, all with little to no tuning or investment of staff. Many monitoring software vendors sell this idea, but it's a myth.

Monitoring isn't just a single, cut-and-dry problem—it's actually a huge problem set. Even limiting the topic to server monitoring, we're still talking about handling metrics and logs for server hardware (everything from the out-of-band controller to the RAID controller to the disks), the operating system, all of the various services running, and the complex interactions between all of them. If you are running a large infrastructure (like I suspect many of you are), then paying attention only to your servers won't get you very far: you'll need to monitor the network infrastructure and the applications too.

Hoping to find a single tool that will do all of that for you is simply delusional.

So what can you do about it?

Monitoring Is Multiple Complex Problems Under One Name

We've already established that monitoring isn't a single problem, so it stands to reason that it can't be solved with a single tool either. Just like a professional mechanic has an entire box of tools, some general and some specialized, so should you:

- If you're trying to profile and monitor your applications at the code level, you might look at APM tools, or instrumenting the application yourself (e.g., StatsD).
- If you need to monitor performance of a cloud infrastructure, you might look at modern server monitoring solutions.
- If you need to monitor for spanning tree topology changes or routing updates, you might look at tools with a network focus.

In any mature environment, you'll fill your toolbox with a set of general and specialized tools.

The Observer Effect Isn't a Problem

The observer effect states that the act of observing a thing causes that thing to change. When it comes to technology, this is often taken to mean that any observation tools are going to place additional load on a system. That's true—but it's not actually a problem.

Let me put this one to rest now: it's 2017, not 1999—your systems can handle the additional load, however minuscule it will be (and it *will* be minuscule).

Some people seem concerned about using an agent at all. Agents aren't a bad thing: how else are you planning to get metrics out of these systems? If you're worried about management and configuration of the agent, you should be using a configuration management tool (if you're not, put this book down and go learn and implement config management). Agentless monitoring is extraordinarily inflexible and will never give you the amount of control and visibility you desire—bite the bullet and you'll never look back.

I've found it's common for people to be afraid of *tool creep*. That is, they are wary of bringing more tools into their environment for fear of increasing complexity. This is a good thing to be wary of, though I think it's less of a problem than most people imagine.

How Many Tools Is Too Many?

How many monitoring tools is too many? Unfortunately, there's no hard-and-fast rule I can give you on this. I've worked with companies supporting only a handful of tools for specific purposes all the way up to large enterprises with over a hundred different tools, many of them overlapping in purpose and function.

The guidance I can provide is this: as few as you need to get the job done. If you have three tools to monitor your database and they all provide the same information, you should consider consolidating. On the other hand, if all three of those tools monitor your databases and provide different information, you're probably fine. Tool fragmentation is only a real problem when the tools don't work together and can't correlate their data.

My advice is to choose tools wisely and consciously, but don't be afraid of adding new tools simply because it's yet another tool. It's a good thing that your network engineers are using tools specialized for their purpose. It's a good thing that your software engineers are using APM tools to dive deep into their code.

In essence, it's desirable that your teams are using tools that solve their problems, instead of being forced into tools that are a poor fit for their needs in the name of "consolidating tools." If everyone is forced to use the same tools, it's unlikely that you're going to have a great outcome, simply due to a poor fit. On the other hand, where you should be rightfully worried is when you have many tools that have an inability to work together. If your systems team can't correlate latency on the network with poor application responsiveness, you should reevaluate your solutions.

What if you want to set some company standards on tools to prevent runaway adoption? In essence, you might have dozens of tools all doing the same thing. In such a case, you're missing out on the benefits that come with standardization: institutional expertise, easier implementation of monitoring, and lower expenses. How would you go about determining if you're in that situation?

It's easy. Well, sort of: you have to start talking to people, and a lot of them. I find it helpful to start an informal conversation with managers of teams and find out what monitoring tools are being used and for what purpose. Make it clear right away that you're not setting out to change how they work—you're gathering information so you can help make their jobs easier later. Forcing change on people is a great way to derail any consolidation effort like this, so keep it light and informal for now. If you're unable to get clear answers, check with accounting: purchase orders and credit card purchases for the past year will reveal both monthly SaaS subscriptions and annual licensing/SaaS subscriptions. Make sure to confirm what you find is actually in use though—you may just find tools that are no longer in use and haven't been cancelled yet.

Avoid Cargo-Culting Tools

There is a story recounted in Richard Feynman's book *Surely You're Joking, Mr. Feynman!* about what Feynman dubbed *cargo cult science*:

> In the South Seas there is a cargo cult of people. During the war they saw airplanes land with lots of good materials, and they want the same thing to happen now. So they've arranged to imitate things like runways, to put fires along the sides of the runways, to make a wooden hut for a man to sit in, with two wooden pieces on his head like headphones and bars of bamboo sticking out like antennas—he's the controller—and they wait for the airplanes to land. They're doing everything right. The form is perfect. It looks exactly the way it looked before. But it doesn't work. No airplanes land. So I call these things cargo cult science, because they follow all the apparent precepts and forms of scientific investigation, but they're missing something essential, because the planes don't land.

Over the years, this observation from the science community has become applied to software engineering and system administration: adopting tools and procedures of more successful teams and companies in the misguided notion that the tools and procedures are what made those teams successful, so they will also make your own team successful in the same ways. Sadly, the cause and effect are backward: the success that team experienced led them to create the tools and procedures, not the other way around.

It's become commonplace for companies to publicly release tools and procedures they use for monitoring their infrastructure and applications. Many of these tools are quite slick and have influenced the development of other monitoring solutions widely used today (for example, Prometheus (*https://prometheus.io*) drew much inspiration from Google's internal monitoring system, Borgmon).

Here's the rub: what you don't see are the many years of effort that went into understanding why a tool or procedure works. Blindly adopting these won't necessarily lead to the same success the authors of those tools and procedures experienced. Tools are a manifestation of ways of working, of assumptions, of cultural and social norms. Those norms are unlikely to map directly to the norms of your own team.

I don't mean to discourage you from adopting tools published by other teams—by all means, do so! Some of them are truly amazing and will change the way you and your colleagues work for the better. Rather, don't adopt them simply because a well-known company uses them. It is important to evaluate and prototype solutions rather than choosing them because someone else uses them or because a team member used them in the past. Make sure the assumptions the tools make are assumptions you and your team are comfortable with and will work well within. Life is too short to suffer with crummy tools (or even great tools that don't fit your workflow), so be sure to really put them through their paces before integrating them into your environment. Choose your tools with care.

Sometimes, You Really Do Have to Build It

When I was growing up, I loved to go through my grandfather's toolbox. It had every tool imaginable, plus some that baffled me as to their use. One day, while helping my grandfather fix something, he suddenly stopped, looking a little perplexed, and began rummaging through the toolbox. Unsatisfied, he grabbed a wrench, a hammer, and a vice. A few minutes later he had created a new tool, built for his specific need. What was once a general-purpose wrench became a specialized tool for solving a problem he never had before. Sure, he could have spent many more hours solving the problem with the tools he had, but creating a new tool allowed him to solve a particular problem in a highly effective manner, in a fraction of the time he might have spent otherwise.

Creating your own specialized tool does have its advantages. For example, one of the first tools many teams build is something to allow the creation of AWS EC2 instances quickly and with all the standards of their company automatically applied. Another example, this one monitoring-related, is a tool I once created: while working with SNMP (which we'll be going into in Chapter 9), I needed a way to comb through a large amount of data and pull out specific pieces of information. No other tool on the market did what I needed, so with a bit of Python, I created a new tool suited for my purpose.

Note that I'm not suggesting you build a completely new monitoring platform. Most companies are not at the point where the ground-up creation of a new platform is a wise idea. Rather, I'm speaking to small, specialized tools.

The Single Pane of Glass Is a Myth

Every *Network Operations Center* (NOC) I've been in has had gargantuan monitors covering the wall, filled with graphs, tables, and other information. I once worked in a NOC (pronounced like "knock") myself that had six 42" monitors spanning the wall, with constant updates on the state of the servers, network infrastructure, and security stance. It's great eye candy for visitors.

However, I've noticed there can often be a misconception around what the *single pane of glass* approach to monitoring means. This approach to monitoring manifests as the desire to have one single *place* to go to look at the state of things. Note that I didn't say one tool or one dashboard—this is crucial to understanding the misconception.

There does not need to be a one-to-one mapping of tools to dashboards. You might use one tool to output multiple dashboards or you might even have multiple tools feeding into one dashboard. More likely, you're going to have multiple tools feeding multiple dashboards. Given that monitoring is a complex series of problems, attempting to shoehorn everything into one tool or dashboard system is just going to hamper your ability to work effectively.

Anti-Pattern #2: Monitoring-as-a-Job

As companies grow, it's common for them to adopt specialized roles for team members. I once worked for a large enterprise organization that had specialized roles for everyone: there was the person who specialized in log collection, there was the person who specialized in managing Solaris servers, and another person whose job it was to create and maintain monitoring for all of it. Three guesses which one was me.

At first glance, it makes sense: create specialized roles so people can focus on doing that function perfectly, instead of being a generalist and doing a mediocre job on everything. However, when it comes to monitoring, there's a problem: how can you build monitoring for a thing you don't understand?

Thus, the anti-pattern: monitoring is not a job—it's a skill, and it's a skill everyone on your team should have to some degree. You wouldn't expect only one member of your team to be the sole person familiar with your config management tool, or how to manage your database servers, so why would you expect that when it comes to monitoring? Monitoring can't be built in a vacuum, as it's a crucial component to the performance of your services.

As you move along your monitoring journey, insist that everyone be responsible for monitoring. One of the core tenets of the DevOps movement is that we're all responsible for production, not just the operations team. Network engineers know best what should be monitored in the network and where the hot spots are. Your software engineers know the applications better than anyone else, putting them in the perfect position to design great monitoring for the applications.

Strive to make monitoring a first-class citizen when it comes to building and managing services. Remember, it's not ready for production until it's monitored. The end result will be far more robust monitoring with great signal-to-noise ratio, and likely far better signal than you've ever had before.

There is a distinction that must be made here, of course: the job of building self-service monitoring tools as a service you provide to another team (commonly called an *observability team*) is a valid and common approach. In these situations, there is a team whose job is to create and cultivate the monitoring tools that the rest of the company relies on. However, this team is not responsible for instrumenting the applications, creating alerts, etc. The anti-pattern I want to caution you against isn't having a person or team responsible for building and providing self-service monitoring tools, but rather, it's having your company shirk the responsibility of monitoring at all by resting it solely on the shoulders of a single person.

Anti-Pattern #3: Checkbox Monitoring

When people tell me that their monitoring sucks, I find that this anti-pattern is usually at the center of it all.

Checkbox monitoring is when you have monitoring systems for the sole sake of saying you have them. Perhaps someone higher up in the organization made it a requirement, or perhaps you suddenly had specific compliance regulations to meet, necessitating a quick monitoring deployment. Regardless of how you got here, the result is the same: your monitoring is ineffective, noisy, untrustworthy, and probably worse than having no monitoring at all.

How do you know if you've fallen victim to this anti-pattern? Here are some common signs:

- You are recording metrics like system load, CPU usage, and memory utilization, but the service still goes down without your knowing why.

- You find yourself consistently ignoring alerts, as they are false alarms more often than not.
- You are checking systems for metrics every five minutes or even less often.
- You aren't storing historical metric data (I'm looking at you, Nagios).

This anti-pattern is commonly found with the previous anti-pattern (monitoring-as-a-job). Since the person(s) setting up monitoring doesn't completely understand how the system works, they often set up the simplest and easiest things and check it off the to-do list.

There are a few things you can do to fix this anti-pattern.

What Does "Working" Actually Mean? Monitor That.

To fix this problem, you first need to understand what it is you're monitoring. What does "working" mean in this context? Talking to the service/app owner is a great place to start.

Are there high-level checks you can perform to verify it's working? For example, if we're talking about a webapp, the first check I would set up is an HTTP GET /. I would record the HTTP response code, expect an HTTP 200 OK response, specific text to be on the page, and the request latency. This one check has given me a wealth of information about whether the webapp is actually working. When things go south, latency might increase while I continue to receive an HTTP 200 response, which tells me there might be a problem. In another scenario, I might get back the HTTP 200, but the text that should be on the page isn't found, which tells me there might be a problem.

Every service and product your company has will have these sorts of high-level checks. They don't necessarily tell you what's wrong, but they're great leading indicators that *something* could be wrong. Over time, as you understand your service/app more, you can add more specific checks and alerts.

OS Metrics Aren't Very Useful—for Alerting

Early in my career as a systems administrator, I went to my lead engineer and told him that the CPU usage on a particular server was quite high, and asked what we should do about it. His response was illuminating for me: "Is the server still doing what it's supposed to?" It was, I told him. "Then there's not really a problem, is there?"

Some services we run are resource-intensive by nature and that's OK. If MySQL is using all of the CPU consistently, but response times are acceptable, then you don't really have a problem. That's why it's far more beneficial to alert on what "working" means as opposed to low-level metrics such as CPU and memory usage.

That isn't to say these metrics aren't useful, of course. OS metrics are critical for diagnostics and performance analysis, as they allow you to spot blips and trends in underlying system behavior that might be impacting performance. 99% of the time, they aren't worth waking someone up over. Unless you have a specific reason to alert on OS metrics, stop doing it.

Collect Your Metrics More Often

In a complex system (like the one you are running), a lot can happen in a few minutes, or even a few seconds. Let's consider an example: imagine latency between two services spikes every 30 seconds, for whatever reason. At a five-minute metric resolution, you would miss the event. Only collecting your metrics every five minutes means you're effectively blind. Opt for collecting metrics *at least* every 60 seconds. If you have a high-traffic system, opt for more often, such as every 30 seconds or even every 10 seconds.

Some people have argued that collecting metrics more often places too much load on the system, which I call baloney. Modern servers and network gear have very high performance and can easily handle the minuscule load more monitoring will place on them.

Of course, keeping high-granularity metrics around on disk for a long period of time can get expensive. You probably don't need to store a year of CPU metric data at 10-second granularity. Make sure you configure a roll-up period that makes sense for your metrics.[1]

The one caveat with this is that many older network devices often have very low performance available to the management cards, causing them to fall over when hit with too many requests for monitoring data (I'm looking at you, Cisco). Be sure to test them in a lab before increasing the polling interval for these.

Anti-Pattern #4: Using Monitoring as a Crutch

I once worked with a team that ran a legacy PHP app. This app had a large amount of poorly written and poorly understood code. As things tended to break, the team's usual response was to add more monitoring around whatever it was that broke. Unfortunately, while this response seems at first glance to be the correct response, it does little to solve the real problem: a poorly built app.

Avoid the tendency to lean on monitoring as a crutch. Monitoring is great for alerting you to problems, but don't forget the next step: fixing the problems. If you find yourself with a finicky service and you're constantly adding more monitoring to it, stop

---

1 Consult the documentation for your metrics tool on roll-up configuration and best practices.

and invest your effort into making the service more stable and resilient instead. More monitoring doesn't fix a broken system, and it's not an improvement in your situation.

Anti-Pattern #5: Manual Configuration

I'm sure we all can agree that automation is awesome. That's why it's surprising to me how often monitoring configuration is manual. The question I never want to hear is "Can you add this to monitoring?"

Monitoring Cloud Architectures Versus Traditional Ones

Monitoring cloud-based architectures differs from traditional (aka static) architectures in one big way: you are monitoring entire *classes* of things, rather than individual things. Monitoring becomes an exercise in analyzing the aggregate of entire groups of systems rather than one or two. Automation is crucial to successfully monitoring a cloud-native architecture.

Your monitoring should be 100% automated. Services should self-register instead of someone having to add them. Whether you're using a tool such as Sensu (*https://sensuapp.org*) that allows for instant self-registration and deregistration of nodes, or using Nagios coupled with config management, monitoring ought to be automatic.

The difficulty in building a well-monitored infrastructure and app without automation cannot be overstated. I'm often called on to consult on monitoring implementations, and in most cases, the team spends more time on configuration than on monitoring. If you cannot quickly configure new checks or nodes, building better monitoring becomes frustrating. After a while, you'll just stop bothering. On the other hand, if it takes only a few minutes to add new checks for every web server in your fleet, you won't be so hesitant to do more of it.

Runbook Abuse

A special note on runbooks, which I talk about in more detail in Chapter 3: a runbook can often be a symptom of inadequate automation. If your runbook is simply a list of steps to take ("Run this command, check this information, run this other command"), then you need more automation. If the alert the runbook is referencing can be solved by simply going through a list of steps, consider automating those steps and having your monitoring tool execute that before alerting you.

Wrap-Up

We learned about five common anti-patterns in monitoring in this chapter:

- Tool obsession doesn't give you better monitoring.
- Monitoring is everyone's job, not a single role on the team or a department.
- Great monitoring is more than checking the box marked "Yep, we have monitoring."
- Monitoring doesn't fix broken things.
- Lack of automation is a great way to ensure you've missed something important.

Now that you know the monitoring anti-patterns to watch out for and how to fix them, you can build positive monitoring habits. If you were to do nothing but fix these five problems in your environment, you'd be in good shape. Of course, who wants to settle for good when they can be great? And for that, we'll need to talk about the inverse of the anti-pattern: the *design pattern*.

## CHAPTER 2

Monitoring Design Patterns

In the last chapter we covered how good intentions can result in a well-meaning train wreck. I certainly don't expect you to have solved all of those problems in your environment by the time you read this chapter, and that's totally OK. Since you can now be mindful of the anti-patterns and work on solving them, you're going to need new solutions for what to do in their place.

This chapter answers that question by presenting four design patterns that, if taken seriously and implemented, will lead you to monitoring nirvana. Let's dig in.

Pattern #1: Composable Monitoring

Composable monitoring is the first pattern of modern monitoring design. The principle is simple: use multiple specialized tools and couple them loosely together, forming a monitoring "platform." This pattern is directly in opposition to the monolithic tools many of you are familiar with, chief among them, Nagios. Composable monitoring can be thought of as the UNIX philosophy in action:

> Write programs that do one thing and do it well. Write programs to work together.
>
> —Doug McIlroy

Back in 2011, conversations about why monitoring was so bad grew around the #monitoringsucks hashtag on Twitter. This grew into #monitoringlove and the founding of the Monitorama conference in Boston. Many, many conversations were had about what could be done to improve things. One of the biggest points raised was that we needed new and better tools. More specialized tools. Composable monitoring as an idea was thus born, and it has grown into a de facto standard in practice. With the rise of tools such as Graphite, Sensu, logstash, and collectd, we can clearly see that tying specialized tools together has resulted in a more flexible and less painful monitoring stack. Even commercial monitoring services, such as Librato, Loggly, and Pingdom, have extensive APIs to control and manage how monitoring is done through them.

One of the biggest perks of composable monitoring is that you are no longer committed long-term to a particular tool or way of doing things. If one tool no longer suits your needs, you can remove it and replace it with another, instead of replacing your entire platform. Such flexibility can lead to a more complex architecture, but the benefits far outweigh the costs.

The Components of a Monitoring Service

If we are to build a monitoring platform from loosely coupled specialized components, we first have to break down what the facets of a monitoring system are. A monitoring service has five primary facets:

- Data collection
- Data storage
- Visualization
- Analytics and reporting
- Alerting

Even if you're using a monolithic tool, you have these components in place—-they're just in a single tool instead of multiple. In order to understand how composable monitoring helps, we'll dig into each component. Each of these components is fairly straightforward in concept but can range from simple to mind-bogglingly complex in practice. Thankfully, we have plenty of options for how complex we make them when it comes to implementation.

Data collection

The data collection component does just that: it collects data. There are two primary ways for data collection to happen: *push* or *pull*. As silly as it sounds, this distinction has yielded more than its fair share of think pieces and conference talks. For those reading this book, the decision isn't that important—use what works for you and move on.

In the pull model, a service will request that a remote node send data about itself. The central service is responsible for scheduling when those requests happen. You are likely familiar with SNMP and Nagios, both of which are pull-based monitoring tools. Some people argue that pull-based is always a bad idea, but I believe it's more nuanced than that. When it comes to monitoring network gear, you're pretty much stuck with SNMP, though that is slowly changing as network hardware vendors come to their senses. Another use case is the /health endpoint pattern in application monitoring, which exposes metrics and health information about an app to an HTTP endpoint, which can be polled by a monitoring service, service discovery tool (such as Consul (*https://www.consul.io*) or etcd (*https://coreos.com/etcd*)), or by a load balancer.

When it comes to metrics, there are some annoying downsides for a pull-based mechanism: a pull model can be difficult to scale, as it requires central systems to keep track of all known clients, handle scheduling, and parse returning data.

In the push model, a client (a server, an application, etc.) *pushes* data to another location. The client may do so on a regular schedule or as events occur. syslog forwarding is a great example of a push model with irregular events, while the popular metrics collection agent collectd is an example of a push model on a regular schedule. A push model is easier to scale in a distributed architecture, such as those in cloud environments, due to the lack of a central poller (coordinating polling schedules across multiple pollers is tricky and you'll still need to maintain a master list of all nodes to poll). Nodes pushing data need only know where to send it, and don't need to worry about underlying implementation of the receiving end. As a result, the push model can have better redundancy and high availability.

Each approach has its own merits and use cases. In my experience, using push-based tools is easier to work with and reason about, but your mileage may vary.

As for what data we may be gathering, we're concerned about two types: metrics and logs.

Metrics. Metrics come in different representations:

Counter
> A counter is an ever-increasing metric. The odometer in your car is an example of a counter. Counters are great for such things as counting the cumulative number of visitors to your website.

> Traffic on a network interface is an example of a counter. Just like the odometer on your car, counters have an upper bound. Once that upper bound is crossed, the counter will "roll over" (or, "wrap") and start over again at zero. A technical example of this is a 32-bit network interface counter. Under 100% load, a 32-bit counter on a 1 Gb interface will wrap in 32 seconds. Thankfully, most operating systems and network devices that implement counters are using 64-bit counters, which will take on the order of years to wrap (4.5 years, in fact). This is mostly only a concern on network gear, which will we go into more in Chapter 9.

Gauge
> A gauge is a point-in-time value. The speedometer in your car is an example of a gauge. The nature of a gauge has one big shortcoming: it doesn't tell you anything about previous values and provides no hints for future values. However, by stor-

ing gauge values in a TSDB, you can retrieve them later and do such things as plot them on a graph. Most metrics you'll be working with are gauges.

Logs. Logs are essentially strings of text with (hopefully) a timestamp associated with them to denote when the event occurred. Logs contain significantly more data than metrics do, and often require some parsing to get information out of them without a human reading through them. Logs come in two types: unstructured and structured.

Most of us are used to dealing with unstructured logs. *Unstructured logs* have no explicit mapping of meaning to a particular field. For example, consider this log entry from NGINX, a popular web server:

```
192.34.63.77 - - [26/Jun/2016:14:06:22 -0400] "GET / HTTP/1.1" 301 184
"-" "Mozilla/5.0 (Windows NT 10.0; WOW64) AppleWebKit/537.36 (KHTML,
like Gecko) Chrome/47.0.2526.111 (StatusCake)" "-"
```

If I were to ask you to tell me what the status code and user agent were, would you immediately know? Semantics in unstructured logs are often implied by order, so if you're unfamiliar with NGINX or web servers, you would have a difficult time answering the question without finding the NGINX documentation.

Let's take this same log entry and turn it into a structured log entry with JSON:

```
{ "remote_addr": "192.34.63.77", "remote_user": "-", "time":
"2016-06-26T14:06:22-04:00", "request": "GET / HTTP/1.1", "status":
"301", "body_bytes_sent": "184", "http_referrer": "-",
"http_user_agent": "Mozilla/5.0 (Windows NT 10.0; WOW64) AppleWebKit/
537.36 (KHTML, like Gecko) Chrome/47.0.2526.111 (StatusCake)",
"http_x_forwarded_for": "-" }
```

As you can see, we've turned our log entry into key-value pairs. Quickly understanding what a field means is so much easier now that semantics are explicit. Even better is that now we can let computers do what computers do and extract the information for us with ease. I encourage you to use structured logging where you can. There are plenty of guides online for switching various services over to use a structured format (JSON is the most popular).[1]

Sometimes Unstructured Logs Are Best

Depending on your use case and tools, it may not make sense to turn your unstructured logs into structured ones. If the logs are low volume, explicitly meant for

---

[1] Here's one guide for switching Apache and NGINX to JSON: *http://bit.ly/2vAWbsX*.

human consumption, and you don't need any tools more complicated than *grep* and *tail*, I would keep your logs unstructured. No need to complicate things unnecessarily.

That said, the majority of your logs probably *should* be structured and sent to a system capable of parsing them.

Log collection can be done in a couple different ways, but the most common (and easiest) is to set up log forwarding on your systems. Every major operating system and logging daemon supports log forwarding, including network gear. Log forwarding allows you to tell your systems to send their logs to another place instead of letting them sit locally on the system. The benefits are obvious, as you can now analyze logs for many systems from a single place instead of logging into multiple systems. On a large fleet of systems, this allows for easy aggregation of similar data for large-scale analysis. For example, consider the scenario where you might have a dozen web servers behind a load balancer. Instead of logging into each of the dozen web servers individually to check logs, log forwarding to a remote logging service allows you to analyze all dozen from a single place, giving you a more complete picture of what your web servers are up to.

If you are writing applications, you should be logging information from them. Most programming frameworks (e.g., Ruby on Rails and Django) have built-in logging capabilities with their own structure, though you can also define your structure. Once the files are on disk, you can easily have the syslog daemon on the server forward these files to a remote service.

Data storage

After collecting the data, you'll need somewhere to store it. Depending on the data type, this might be a specialized solution.

Metrics, being time series, are usually stored in a *Time Series Database* (TSDB). A TSDB is a specialized sort of database designed for storing time series data, which is fundamentally key-value pairs made up of a timestamp (when the measurement was taken) and a value. We refer to the key-value pair as a *datapoint*. You may already be familiar with two common TSDBs: Round Robin Database (RRD) and Graphite's Whisper. There are many others in various stages of maturity.

Many TSDBs "roll up" or "age out" data after a certain time period. This means that as the data gets older, multiple datapoints are summarized into a single datapoint. A common rollup method is averaging, though some tools support other methods such as summing datapoints.

For example, assume we had a rollup schedule of the following: metrics are collected every 60 seconds from a node, stored at native resolution (60 seconds) for 1 day, then summarized to 5 minutes after 3 days. This means that there would be 86,400 datapoints for the past 24 hours of metrics, but only 864 datapoints for the next 3 days. This occurs by averaging the values for every datapoint in a five-minute period into one datapoint. Metric rollup occurs as a result of compromises: storing native resolution for metrics gets very expensive for disks, both in storage and in the time it takes to read all of those datapoints from disk for use in a graph.

Many people are of the opinion that rolling up data is undesirable. Certainly, for some kinds of metrics, this could be true, but for the vast majority of operational data, do you really care what the CPU was doing at a 60-second granularity last week? Probably not. When it comes to operational data, you are far more concerned with recent events, and only with a general idea of older trends.

Log storage comes in a two different flavors. Some systems store the data as simple flat files. If you've ever told `rsyslog` to forward to another syslog receiver for remote storage, you've seen this in action. More advanced solutions store the log files in a search engine (such as Elasticsearch). If you actually want to use your logs, you will be interested in the latter. Most logging platforms will include the storage component, making this somewhat transparent.

While metric storage is inexpensive, storing logs can get expensive. It's not uncommon to generate terabytes worth of data per day. There's not a magic solution to this problem, but compression and retention policies can help.

Visualization

Everyone loves charts and dashboards, making them the most visible component to your monitoring platform. If you are using a monolithic tool (e.g., Nagios and Solar-Winds' NPM) then you're basically stuck with the dashboard provided, with little (if any) room for building your own stuff. If you're using tools built for composability, you have far more options.

Why would you want to build your own frontend? Having tons of data is fine, but it's useless if you can't make sense of it in a way that suits you and your team. What good is a bunch of metrics with cluttered, confusing dashboards? A driving principle behind great monitoring is that you should be building things in a way that works best for your environment.

There are lots of dashboard products and frameworks out there, such as Grafana (*https://grafana.com/*) and Smashing (*https://github.com/Smashing/smashing*).

When it comes to visualization, an entire book could written on the topic. Oh, wait a minute, many great books *have* been written on the topic!

Edward Tufte's *The Visual Display of Quantitative Information* (Graphics Press) and Stephen Few's *Information Dashboard Design* (Analytics Press) are excellent resources for going deeper into the world of data visualization. I cannot do these works justice in a short section such as this, so if you're interested in the world of visualization, I strongly recommend reading them.

The most common visualization for time series data is the line graph (also called a strip chart), but there are certainly other representations that can be useful. Displaying data in a table format, a bar graph, a singular number, or even straight text can all have their value. For the most part, you'll be working with line graphs in ops/software engineering.

But for the Love of God, Don't Use a Pie Chart

The primary use of a pie chart is for a snapshot-in-time visualization. It doesn't contain any context about history or trends is and therefore best used for data that doesn't change often. The most common use for a pie chart is to show data in relation to the whole, but even still, a bar chart is often a better visualization for that purpose.

Speaking of dashboards, what makes a great one? Useful dashboards have different perspectives and scopes. A great dashboard answers questions you have at a particular time. You might have one dashboard that shows only a high-level overview of every major functionality and service of your company (WAN, LAN, applications, etc.), while you might have more dashboards for each of those major services. You might even have more dashboards for different aspects of those services.

The best dashboards focus on displaying the status of a single service (e.g., the internal email system or the corporate network routing topology) or one product (e.g., a single app). These dashboards are most effective if they are created and maintained by the people who understand the service the best. For example, if you have an internal email service, have the admins for that service create the dashboards for it.

Analytics and Reporting

For some types of monitoring data, it can be helpful to go beyond a simple visualization and into the realms of analytics and reporting.

One of the most common use cases here is determining and reporting on *service-level availability* (SLA) of your applications and services. An SLA is an agreement between you and your customer (whether that's an external, paying customer or another internal team) regarding the expected availability of your application/service, typically determined month by month.[2] Depending on the agreement, there might be contractual penalties for not meeting the SLA. SLAs with no penalty clause are generally considered to be more of a "target to hit." Penalty or not, it's important that your monitoring data is complete and accurate so you're able to effectively report on availability.

SLAs Are (Mostly) Hopes and Lies

I'm cynical about SLAs. The penalty for not meeting an SLA is just a refund, though at worst, you might lose a customer. Many enterprise software contracts contain unrealistic SLA expectations (of the "no downtime ever" variety), making the whole game suspect.

Availability is referred to by the number of *nines*. That is, 99% is *two nines*, while 99.99% is *four nines*.[3] In a simple infrastructure, the math is straightforward: determine how much downtime you had and compute that in terms of an availability percentage. The formula for this is equally simple: $a = uptime\ /\ total\ time$, where *total time* is the time the component was both up and down. The resulting a is a percentage measurement of availability. Let's look at an example:

If your app ran for a complete month (43,800 minutes) and experienced 93 minutes of downtime, then the availability would be 99.7% (43,707 (uptime) / 43,800). Pretty simple, right?

Did You Spot the Sampling Error?

This calculation is actually naive and has a problem that's easy to overlook: a sampling error.

According to the *Nyquist-Shannon sampling theorem* (*http://bit.ly/ 2i2kBmv*), to measure an outage of two minutes, you must be collecting data in minute-long intervals. Thus, to measure availability down to one second, you must be collecting data at sub-second intervals. This is just one more reason why achieving accurate SLA reporting better than 99% is so difficult.

---

2 I encourage you to track this information even if you aren't required to. It's helpful to understand your own reliability in order to improve it.

3 I've included a full chart of availability numbers in Appendix B.

Well, not quite. You might notice that computing uptime and total time in a complex architecture is tricky, and you would be right. In order to determine the required numbers, you would have to compute them for each and every component that your app depends on. If components of the app have redundancy, you have two options: accuracy or ease.

If you want to be completely accurate in your availability calculations and reporting, you'll need to calculate the availability of each redundant component, then calculate the availability of the component as a whole. This math can get more complex than what you're probably interested in, and in my opinion, isn't that helpful.

Instead, I recommend calculating the availability of the component as a whole and ignoring the availability of the underlying redundant components. The calculation is much simpler and more directly answers what you're really looking for anyway.

An oft-overlooked point about availability is when your app has dependency components: your service can only be as available as the underlying components on which it is built. For example, did you know that AWS EC2 only provides a 99.95% SLA for a single region? (*https://aws.amazon.com/ec2/sla/*) That's about four hours of downtime a year. If you're running your infrastructure in AWS in a single region, you can't promise a higher SLA than that without potentially violating the SLA. Likewise if your underlying network is unreliable, the servers and applications higher in the stack can't possibly be more reliable than the network.

A final point before moving on: 100% availability is unrealistic. The downtime that maps to nine nines (99.9999999% availability) is roughly *31 seconds of downtime per year*. Recall that even AWS EC2 has an SLA guarantee of fewer than four nines, and there's a good chance AWS invests more into the reliability of EC2 than your company makes in revenue per year. Each additional nine of availability has significantly more cost associated with it, and the investment often isn't worth it: many customers can't tell the difference between 99% and 99.9%.

Alerting

I have found that many people seem to build monitoring without understanding its purpose. They seem to believe that the driving purpose of a monitoring system is to alert you when things go wrong. While older monitoring systems like Nagios certainly lead you to that conclusion, monitoring has a higher purpose. As a friend of mine once said:

> Monitoring is for asking questions.
>
> —Dave Josephsen, *Monitorama 2016*

That is, monitoring doesn't exist to generate alerts: alerts are just one possible outcome. With this in mind, remember that every metric you collect and graph does not need to have a corresponding alert.

Pattern #2: Monitor from the User Perspective

By now, you're probably itching to start building things, but where do you start? Your app and infrastructure are complex, with lots and lots of moving parts—failure could happen anywhere!

You're totally right. There are a lot of places we are going to need to instrument things, but there's one perfect place to start: the users (Figure 2-1).

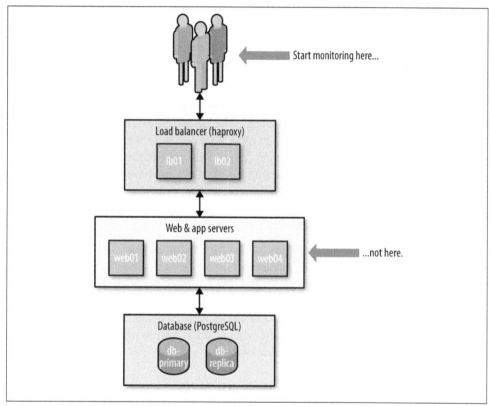

Figure 2-1. Start monitoring as close to the user as possible

The best place to add monitoring first is at the point(s) users interact with your app. A user doesn't care about the implementation details of your app, such as how many Apache nodes you're running or how many workers are available for jobs. Your users care about whether the application works. As such, you want visibility from their perspective first.

One of the most effective things to monitor is simply HTTP response codes (especially of the HTTP 5xx variety). Monitoring request times (aka latency) after that is also useful. Neither of these will tell you *what* is wrong, only that something *is* and that it's impacting users.

By monitoring from the user's perspective first, you begin to free yourself from the worry of caring about individual nodes. If your database server's CPU has started to spike, but the user isn't impacted, do you really have a problem?

Now, I'm not suggesting that this is the only place you instrument your app. You should be starting with the user, but you should quickly expand your efforts to instrumenting components, such as those web nodes and worker nodes. Go as deep and wide as you want, but always be asking asking yourself, "How will these metrics show me the user impact?"

Pattern #3: Buy, Not Build

We discussed the anti-pattern of *tool obsession* in Chapter 1. This design pattern is essentially the direct answer to that anti-pattern.

I've noticed a natural progression of monitoring tooling and culture as it matures within a company.

Companies often start off running purely SaaS services. This allows them to quickly get monitoring up and running, and gives them the ability to focus their efforts on building a great product.

At some point (a point that comes at different times for every company and team), monitoring is brought in-house. Sometimes it happens for financial reasons, sometimes it happens because the SaaS services are no longer meeting the needs of a growing product. The tools they transition to are the well-known FOSS monitoring tools, such as Graphite, InfluxDB, Sensu, and Prometheus.

A small group of companies will eventually outgrow even those and set out to build their own custom platforms, tailored specifically for the unique concerns and needs of their company. For example, Netflix, Dropbox, and Twitter are all in that final group.

There is often some overlap and mixing of the stages (e.g., you might have a custom metrics platform but use a SaaS logging service), but the important part here is that your first effort at monitoring probably shouldn't be jumping right to building an in-house platform if you're not already reasonably mature in your monitoring. You progress because the tools no longer serve your needs and you've outgrown them. If you have no monitoring or poor monitoring right now, you should put more work into the fundamentals of monitoring things and spend less time worrying about your tools.

I am a big proponent of SaaS solutions for many things. It's my belief that within five years, it will be considered a no-brainer to use SaaS as your monitoring solution. Here's why.

It's Cheaper

What goes into building your own monitoring, whether it's made of FOSS or home-grown tools? You will have to consider the cost of FTEs (full-time employees) to build it and maintain it over time, the lost opportunity cost of those FTEs working on a monitoring system instead of something else, the time to create and maintain documentation for the service, the time to train users on your internal tools, and the operational complexity costs stemming from having a mission-critical service running in-house.

Let's take an example case:[4]

- Average cost of an FTE (salary + benefits + overhead): $150,000
- Number of engineers: 3
- Time to build a decent solution (reliable, scalable, documentation, training): 4 weeks
- Maintenance time: 20 hours a month

With these numbers, it will cost you $35,000 in raw engineering time to build a solution, plus another (roughly) $18,750 per year in maintenance. But don't forget opportunity cost: three engineers spending a month on building a monitoring platform means three engineers spending a month on something that doesn't generate any revenue for your company.

Opportunity cost is hard to quantify due to different roles and business needs. For example, unless your company manages networks for its customers, your network engineers are probably not as crucial to revenue generation as a software engineer at a SaaS company would be. Use your best judgment.

By comparison, a great SaaS monitoring solution will cost most companies between $6,000/yr and $9,000/yr. This seems like a big number, but you really do get quite a bit of bang for your buck.

You're (Probably) Not an Expert at Architecting These Tools

You are probably not an expert at building and maintaining a high-throughput, mission-critical monitoring service. And even if you are, is it really the best use of

---

4 These numbers are very rough estimates.

your time?[5] Many of us remember running our own mail servers and DNS servers, but few of us do that anymore thanks to the rise of SaaS solutions. SaaS solutions allow you to buy dedicated expertise thrown at a specific problem domain, at a price much cheaper than you can do yourself. Amazon is probably way better at running large-scale, highly-available infrastructure than you are, so it's a no-brainer to consider them as a solution-provider. Likewise with Gmail/Google Apps.

SaaS Allows You to Focus on the Company's Product

Using SaaS tools is easier and quicker to get up and running with. If you move quickly, it may take a few days to have a workable in-house solution. You'll be missing any decent user documentation, high-availability, or any real automation, but it'll be workable. On the other hand, SaaS allows you to have a working solution within minutes, and you get all of those things you were missing for free, right from the start.

No, Really, SaaS Is Actually Better

Of course, I've heard plenty of objections to using SaaS for monitoring, but frankly, most of them aren't very good. The only two rational reasons for not using SaaS I've run across across:

1. You really have outgrown it. This is far less common than you might imagine.[6]
2. Security/compliance reasons. Despite even governments making use of SaaS for many services, getting into an argument with your corporate auditors is usually a losing proposition. Many companies resolve this by documenting what's being sent in the logs and never sending any sensitive data to the SaaS service. Your mileage may vary.

By far the most common reason for people not wanting to use SaaS comes down to the perceived cost, which we covered a couple sections ago. As your infrastructure and applications grow, so too does the effort required for monitoring them. However, the time required for growing on-premises monitoring tends to outpace that for SaaS, leading to paying $120,000/yr for SaaS. This causes some people to freak out and staff a team for building their own monitoring. These teams are usually four to five people

---

5 Exceptions made for those whose products are monitoring services. More power to you, in that case.

6 There are some well-known, large companies that have gone from on-premises monitoring tools to SaaS, precisely because running it themselves cost too much money and engineering time. Keep that datapoint in mind.

and cost between \$600,000/yr and \$750,000/yr in just staff. The short answer is that if you're using SaaS, you've probably not outgrown it.[7]

Most people railing against using SaaS for monitoring are doing so out of bias, conscious or unconscious, and not out of any technical or financial reason.

Pattern #4: Continual Improvement

People look up to progressive companies like Google, Facebook, Twitter, Netflix, and Etsy and marvel at the amazing things they've done with monitoring. Countless blogs have been written to talk about how advanced monitoring is at these companies. However, people seem to forget that it took years for each of those companies to get to where they are today. Each of them has retired tools and built new ones as things changed and matured in their organizations.

While you probably aren't responsible for building a world-class monitoring service at a company as large and mature as these, your efforts to improve monitoring will change over time, and you aren't going to be at a world-class level tomorrow and not even a year from now. Even if you are doing well, you will find yourself completely rearchitecting your monitoring every two or three years as your needs change and the industry evolves.

In essence, world-class isn't achieved in a week, but rather, over months and years of consistent attention and improvement. You're in this for the long haul.

Wrap-Up

We've covered the four primary design patterns in this chapter:

- Composable monitoring is more effective than monoliths.
- Monitoring from the user's perspective first yields more effective visibility.
- Opt for buying your monitoring tools if at all possible, instead of building them yourself.
- Always be improving.

While certainly not an exhaustive list, applying these four will get you further along to a great monitoring platform than most companies.

---

7 Some very large companies are still using SaaS for monitoring: Airbnb, Pinterest, Yelp, Target—the list goes on.

Now that you've got these patterns available to you, let's move on to a specific topic that's easy to screw up, hard to get right, and likely represents much of your pain in monitoring: alert design.

## CHAPTER 3

Alerts, On-Call, and Incident Management

Alerting is one of the most crucial parts of monitoring that you will want to get right. For whatever reason, infrastructure likes to go sideways in the middle of the night. Why is it always 3 a.m.? Can't I have an outage at 2 p.m. on a Tuesday? Without alerts, we'd all have to be staring at graphs all day long, every day. With the multitude of things that could possibly go wrong, and the ever-increasing complexity of our systems, this simply isn't tenable.

So, alerts. We can all agree that alerting is an important function of a monitoring system. However, sometimes we forget that the purpose of monitoring isn't solely to send us alerts. Remember our definition:

> Monitoring is the action of observing and checking the behavior and outputs of a system and its components over time.

Alerts are just one way we accomplish this goal.

Great alerting is harder than it seems. System metrics tend to be spike-y, so alerting on raw datapoints tends to produce lots of false alarms. To get around that problem, a rolling average is often applied to the data to smooth it out (for example, five minutes worth of datapoints averaged into one datapoint), which unfortunately causes us to lose granularity, resulting in occasionally missing important events. There's just no winning, is there?

One of the other reasons alerting is so difficult to do well is because you often want alerts them going to a human, and we humans have limited attention. You'd rather spend it on problems of your choosing and not on the monitoring system sending you a text that something is on fire. Every time you get an alert, a little bit more of your attention is claimed by the monitoring system.

In this chapter, we'll cover a few tips on creating better alerts, the trials and tribulations of on-call, and close out with a bit about incident management and postmortems.

What Makes a Good Alert?

With your multitude of alerts that sometimes are helpful, sometimes aren't, and sometimes simply make no sense, how should you reconstruct them to be good? What does a good alert even look like?

Before we can answer that question, let's make a distinction. I've found that when people talk about alerts, they really mean two different things, depending on the context:

Alerts meant to wake someone up
> These require action to be taken immediately or else the system will go down (or continue to be down). This might mean phone calls, text messages, or alarms. Example: all your web servers are unavailable, and your company's main site is no longer reachable.

Alerts meant as an FYI
> These require no immediate action, but someone ought to be informed that they occurred. Example: an overnight backup job failed.

The latter may lead to the former. For example, if your systems are capable of auto-healing, then an auto-healing action might just be a message dropped in a log file. If the auto-healing fails, then you might send a message to the on-call person, expecting immediate action.

For our purposes, the second type of alert isn't actually an alert: it's a message. We're going to be talking mainly about the former here. An alert should evoke a sense of urgency and require action from the person receiving that alert. Everything else can essentially be a log entry, a message dropped in your internal chat room, or an auto-generated ticket.

So with that understanding, we're back the original question: what makes a good alert? I've rounded up six practices I think are key to building great alerts:

- Stop using email for alerts.
- Write runbooks.
- Arbitrary static thresholds aren't the only way.
- Delete and tune alerts.
- Use maintenance periods.

- Attempt self-healing first.

Let's dig deeper into how these impact your alerting strategy and how you can leverage them for improvement.

Stop Using Email for Alerts

An email isn't going to wake someone up, nor should you expect that it would. Sending alerts to email is also a great way to overwhelm everyone with noise, which will lead to alert fatigue.

What should do you do instead? Think about what sorts of use cases each alert will have. I've found they fall into one of three categories:

Response/action required immediately
> Send this to your pager, whether it's an SMS, PagerDuty, or what-have-you. This is an actual alert, per our definition.

Awareness needed, but immediate action not required
> I like to send these to internal chat rooms. Some teams have built small webapps to receive and store these for review with great success. You *could* send these to email, but be careful—it's easy to overwhelm an inbox. The other options are usually better.

Record for historical/diagnostic purposes
> Send the information to a log file.

Logging Your Alerts

It's important to retain logs of your alerts so you can report on them later. Being able to report on alerts will help you understand what parts of your application/service are causing you the most trouble and where you should focus your efforts. It will also aid in reporting on your SLAs.

With proper attention given to the purpose and response required of the alert, you can easily lower the noise level of every alert you have.

Write Runbooks

A runbook is a great way to quickly orient yourself when an alert fires. In more complex environments, not everyone on the team is going to have knowledge about every system, and runbooks are a great way to spread that knowledge around.

A good runbook is written for a particular service and answers several questions:

- What is this service, and what does it do?
- Who is responsible for it?
- What dependencies does it have?
- What does the infrastructure for it look like?
- What metrics and logs does it emit, and what do they mean?
- What alerts are set up for it, and why?

For every alert, include a link to your runbook for that service. When someone responds to the alert, they will open the runbook and understand what's going on, what the alert means, and potential remediation steps.

 As with many good things, runbooks can be easy to abuse. If your remediation steps for an alert are as simple as copy-pasting commands, then you've started to abuse runbooks. You should automate that fix or resolve the underlying issue, then delete the alert entirely. A runbook is for when human judgment and diagnosis is necessary to resolve something.

I've included an example runbook in Appendix A.

Arbitrary Static Thresholds Aren't the Only Way

Nagios got all of us used to the idea of using arbitrary static thresholds for alert criteria, and this is our loss. Not every situation has a warning and critical state that makes sense (I'd argue that most don't). Furthermore, there are a lot of situations where alerting on such things as "datapoint has crossed X" isn't useful at all. For example, the quintessential case for this is disk usage: if I have a static threshold set at "free space under 10%," then I'm going to miss a disk quickly growing in usage from 11% used to 80% used overnight. You know, that kind of thing is something I'd really want to know about, but my static threshold wouldn't tell me.

There are plenty of other options available here. For example, using a percent change/ derivative would handle our disk usage problem nicely by telling us "disk usage has grown by 50% overnight."

With a bit more capable metrics infrastructure (e.g., Graphite), we could even apply some statistics to the problem, using various approaches such as moving averages, confidence bands, and standard deviation. We'll go into more about statistics and how they could be applied in Chapter 4.

Delete and Tune Alerts

Noisy alerts suck. Noisy alerts cause people to stop trusting the monitoring system, which leads people to ignoring it entirely. How many times have you looked at an alert and thought, "I've seen that alert before. It'll clear itself up in a few minutes, so I don't need to do anything"?

The middle ground between high-signal monitoring and low-signal monitoring is treacherous. This is the area where you're getting lots of alerts, some actionable and some not, but it's not to the point that you don't trust the monitoring. Over time, this leads to *alert fatigue*.

Alert fatigue occurs when you are so exposed to alerts that you become desensitized to them. Alerts should (and do!) cause a small adrenaline rush. You think to yourself, "Oh crap! A problem!" Having such a response 10 times a week, for months on end, results in long-term alert fatigue and staff burnout. The human response time slows down, alerts may start getting ignored, sleep is impacted—sound familiar yet?

The solution to alert fatigue is simple on its face: fewer alerts. In practice, this isn't so easy. There are a number of ways to reduce the amount of alerts you're getting:

1. Go back to the first tip: do all your alerts require someone to act?
2. Look at a month's worth of history for your alerts. What are they? What were the actions? What was the impact of each one? Are there alerts that can simply be deleted? What about modifying the thresholds? Could you redesign the underlying check to be more accurate?
3. What automation can you build to make the alert obsolete entirely?

With just a little bit of work, you'll find that your alert noise will be cut back significantly.

Use Maintenance Periods

If you need to do work on a service, and you expect it to trigger an alert (e.g., due to it being down), then set that alert into a maintenance period. Most monitoring tools support the concept, which is a simple one: if you're working on the thing that alert is watching, and you know your work is going to cause an interruption, there's no sense in having the alert go off. An alert firing is just distraction, especially for your teammates who may not immediately know that you're working on it.

Be careful not to silence too many alerts. I can't even begin to count the number of times that I've been working on something and found a previously unknown dependency that caused some other service to start to have problems. Such a scenario is actually desirable, as it reveals things about your infrastructure that you may not have known before, or it can warn you that something might be going sideways with the maintenance work you're doing. Issuing a wide, blanket silence can cause more problems than it solves.

Attempt Automated Self-Healing First

If the most common action needed on an alert is to perform a known and documented series of steps which usually fixes the problem, why not let a computer do the work? Auto-healing is a great approach to avoiding alert fatigue, and when you're managing a large environment, it's not really optional (hiring more staff gets expensive!).

Auto-Healing Embedded Devices

I once had a few dozen small, embedded computers living in places no computer should ever live, such as on roofs, in trees, or the side of a dirt road. They were rather simple sensor devices with two externally accessible interfaces: SNMP and a (very) basic CLI accessible over SSH. Due to the design, the SNMP engine had a tendency to become unresponsive, but the system itself was still running. The fix for this was to log in to the sensor via SSH and restart it, which solved the problem (until the next time it died). This happened on a regular basis, usually two to three times a week. We wanted to know when they stopped responding to SNMP queries immediately (the data collected via SNMP was the entire reason for their existence), but it was getting tiresome to be woken up about it.

With such a simple and straightforward fix to my failing sensor devices, surely I could devise a better solution to this problem.

I came up with a simple method of attempting auto-healing: I first set up a check that detected when SNMP failed (by grabbing any OID and watching for a timeout, while also confirming that the device was accessible via ICMP). If SNMP failed but the device was still on the network, a script logged into the sensor device and restarted it. This worked perfectly: the sensor came back online in a matter of seconds and everything worked again. Most importantly, no one was being woken up over something that could be fixed automatically.

There are several ways you can implement auto-healing, but the most common and straightforward approach is to simply implement any standardized fix into code and let your monitoring system execute the script instead of notifying a human. If the problem wasn't resolved via an auto-healing attempt, *then* send an alert.

On-Call

Ah, good old on-call. Many of you reading this book have probably been on-call at some point in your career, even if it was unofficial. For those that haven't, on-call is where you are expected to be available to respond to pages about things going wrong. If that's you at all times, you're always on-call (this is bad, but we'll talk about that later).

For those with on-call experience, you know how terrible on-call can be.[1] You're plagued by false alarms, unclear alerts, and constant firefighting. After a few months, you start experiencing the effects of burnout: irritability, sleep deprivation, anxiety, and more.

It doesn't have to be this way, though, and I want to show you how to fix it. While we can't avoid computers doing silly things in the middle of the night, we can avoid getting needlessly woken up about it. Let's talk about what we can do about it.

Fixing False Alarms

False alarms, for many us, are just an everyday fact of life when it comes to monitoring. 100% accuracy in alerting is a really hard problem—one that is still unsolved. While tuning alerts isn't always easy, many of you will be able to cut false alarms by an appreciable amount. At any rate, even if you never achieve 100% accuracy, you should still strive for it.

Here's an easy way to always tune the alarms: as part of the duties of the person on-call, compile a list of every alert that fired for the previous day. Go through them and ask yourself how the alert's signal can be improved, or if the alert can be deleted entirely. Do this every day you are on-call and soon you'll be in much better shape than when you started.

Cutting Down on Needless Firefighting

Sometimes it's not a signal problem, and the alerts are legit. Except, there's dozens of them a day, and they're *all* legit. You have an excessive firefights problem. We talked about this back in Chapter 1.

---

1 It's *not* a universal truth that on-call sucks. Many companies have amazing and effective on-call experiences. It takes a lot of work to get there.

To quote a colleague who made an apt observation with monitoring, "You gotta fix your shit."

Monitoring doesn't *fix* anything. *You* need to fix things after they break. To get out of firefighting mode, you must spend time and effort on building better underlying systems. More resilient systems have less show-stopping failures, but you'll only get there by putting in the effort on the underlying problems.

There are two effective strategies to get into this habit:

1. Make it the duty of on-call to work on systems resiliency and stability during their on-call shift when they aren't fighting fires.

2. Explicitly plan for systems resiliency and stability work during the following week's sprint planning/team meeting (you are doing those, right?), based on the information collected from the previous on-call week.

I've seen both methods work successfully, so I'd recommend trying both and seeing which one works better for your team.

Building a Better On-Call Rotation

You've no doubt experienced the unofficial on-call: instead of a formal designation of when you are on-call and when you are not, you were simply always on call. Always being on-call is a great way to burn people out (as I'm sure you already know!), and this is why on-call rotations are a great idea. They're a tried-and-true method of managing on-call response.

Here's how a simple rotation might work. Let's say you have Sarah, Kelly, Jack, and Rich on your team. You set up a four-week rotation, whereby each of them is on-call for one week, starting on Wednesday at 10 a.m. and ending one week later. This rotates through in a specified order until everyone has been on-call for one week and off on-call for three, then repeats itself.

A schedule like this works pretty well and is a great start if you don't have a rotation schedule already.

It's important to start the on-call rotation during the workweek instead of tying it directly to a calendar week. This allows your team to do an on-call handoff: the person coming off on-call discusses with the person going on-call what's in-flight that needs attention, any patterns noticed during the week, etc. I've been on teams where we did handoff at 9 a.m. on Monday morning and others where we did it in the afternoon on Wednesdays—I'd pick whatever day and time works best for your team. If you're not sure, go with Wednesday at 10 a.m.

Follow-the-Sun Rotations

Once your company is large enough, something you can take advantage of is a *follow-the-sun* (FTS) rotation. Instead of a rotation consisting of, say, six people all from one office, you can split the rotation across time zones. For example, a London-based engineer can be on-call during their work hours and handoff to a Los Angeles–based engineer when the UK day ends. Even better is distributing the rotation across Europe, the United States, and Asia-Pacific (e.g., London, Los Angeles, and Sydney). FTS rotations allow you to have full on-call coverage with no one being on-call during their nights. One big downside to FTS rotations is the significant increase in communication overhead. Handing off on-call becomes more difficult, so make sure you have solid processes and communication channels in place.

One question that comes up often about on-call schedules is whether you should have a backup on-call person or not, in addition to the primary on-call person. For most teams, I advise against this unless you have a suitably large team. Having a primary and a backup puts a person on-call for two rotations during the cycle. If you only have a team of four people and use one-week rotations, that means everyone is on-call for two weeks of the month—brutal!

Even if the backup isn't called, they're still required to do all the normal primary on-call things: be near a computer with internet, be sober, and so forth, and that just isn't fair to them (it will also lead to quicker burnout).

This isn't to say that the on-call person is all alone: you do absolutely need escalation paths available for issues beyond the knowledge and capability of the on-call person to solve. My caution has more to do with expecting everyone to always be available, regardless of whether they are officially on-call or not.

Now, I know what you're thinking: what if primary on-call doesn't respond to the alert? That's fine. It's the *job* of the on-call person to respond to alerts, and people are more responsible than they're often given credit for. If you have a consistent problem with your on-call not responding to alerts, you've got a different problem. Otherwise, I wouldn't worry about it.

That brings us to another point: how many people do you need for an effective on-call rotation schedule? That depends on two factors: how busy your on-call tends to be and how much time you want to give people between on-call shifts.

On-call shifts with only two or three incidents a week can be considered light—what you should be aiming for. The more incidents you have on a regular basis, the more time off you should give between rotations. As for how much time off between shifts, for a normal shift (such as the example I gave), I recommend three weeks between on-call shifts for each person. Assuming you have only a single primary on-call, that means you're looking at a team of four people. If you want a backup rotation as well, then you need eight people on the schedule.

I strongly encourage you to put software engineers into the on-call rotation as well. The idea behind this is to avoid the "throw-it-over-the-wall" version of software engineering. If software engineers are aware of the struggles that come up during on-call, and they themselves are part of that rotation, then they are incentivized to build better software. There's also a more subtle reason here: empathy. Putting software engineers and operations engineers together in some way increases empathy for each other, and it's awfully hard to be upset at someone you genuinely understand and like.

Lastly, augment your on-call with tools such as PagerDuty, VictorOps, OpsGenie, etc. These tools help you build and maintain escalation paths and schedules, and can automatically record your incidents for you for later review. I try to avoid recommending specific tools in this book, but when it comes to tools that help on-call, I really cannot recommend these enough.

On-Call Compensation

I would also consider two compensation-related things for your on-call people:

1. Give a PTO day immediately following the end of an on-call shift. On-call can be nerve-wracking and a day to recuperate is well deserved.

2. Pay your team extra for their on-call shift. It's standard practice in the medical profession for on-call to receive additional pay for on-call shifts, ranging from an additional \$2/hr for nurses (*http://bit.ly/2lf6XBm*) up to \$2,000/day for neurosurgeons (*http://bit.ly/2ixJL05*).

On-call negatively impacts many parts of life, including sleep quality, time with family, and more. Additional compensation for the worst part of our industry only seems fair.

With some work, you can significantly improve your on-call experience for everyone involved.

Incident Management

Incident management is a formal way of handling issues that arise. There are several frameworks out there for the tech world, with one of the most popular coming from ITIL (*http://www.bmc.com/guides/itil-incident-management.html*):

> An unplanned interruption to an IT service or reduction in the quality of an IT service.
>
> —ITIL 2011

ITIL's process for incident management looks something like this:

1. Incident identification
2. Incident logging
3. Incident categorization
4. Incident prioritization
5. Initial diagnosis
6. Escalation, as necessary, to level 2 support
7. Incident resolution
8. Incident closure
9. Communication with the user community throughout the life of the incident

Despite the stilted presentation of it, a formal, consistent method for detecting and responding to incidents provides a certain rigor and discipline to a team. For most teams, formal methods such as this are overkill. However, what if we took the preceding ITIL process and simplified it, to not be so heavyweight?

1. Incident identification (monitoring identifies a problem).
2. Incident logging (monitoring automatically opens a ticket for the incident).
3. Incident diagnosis, categorization, resolution, and closure (on-call troubleshoots, fixes the problem, resolves the ticket with comments and additional data).
4. Communications throughout the event as necessary.
5. After the incident is resolved, come up with remediation plans for building in more resiliency.

Hey, that's not so bad. In fact, I'd bet that a lot of you are doing something very similar to this already, and that's great. There is value in establishing your incident response as an internal standard, formal procedure for handling incidents: incidents are logged and followed-up on consistently; your users, management, and customers get more transparency and insight into what's going on; and your team can start to spot patterns and hot spots in the app and infrastructure.

For most incidents that are resolved quickly, this process works well. What about for incidents that are actual outages and last longer than a few minutes? In that case, a well-defined set of roles becomes crucial. Each of these roles has a singular function and they should not be doing double-duty:

Incident commander (IC)
This person's job is to make decisions. Notably, they are not performing any remediation, customer or internal communication, or investigation. Their job is

to oversee the outage investigation and that's it. Often, the on-call person adopts the IC role at the start of the incident. Sometimes the IC role is handed off to someone else, especially if the person on-call is better suited for another role.

Scribe

The scribe's job is to write down what's going on. Who's saying what and when. What decisions are being made? What follow-up items are being identified? Again, this role should not be performing any investigation or remediation.

Communication liaison

This role communicates status updates to stakeholders, whether they are internal or external. In a sense, they are the sole communication point between people working on the incident and people demanding to know what's going on. One facet of this role is to prevent stakeholders (e.g., managers) from interfering with the incident by directly asking those working on resolving the incident for status updates.

Subject matter experts (SMEs)

These are the people actually working on the incident.

 One common anti-pattern I've seen with incident management roles is for them to follow the day-to-day hierarchical structure of the team or company. For example, the manager of the team is always the IC. The incident management roles do not need to resemble the day-to-day team roles. In fact, I encourage you to have the team's manager act as communication liaison rather than IC, and allow an engineer on the team to act as IC. These are often a much better fit, as it allows the manager to protect the team from interruption and it puts decision-making power in a person who is best suited to assess risk and trade-offs.

This is only a brief overview of incident management, but if you're interested in learning more about the topic, I recommend reading PagerDuty's Incident Response documentation (*https://response.pagerduty.com/*).

Postmortems

I want to devote some special attention to step five from the simplified incident response process above. After an incident has occurred, it's always advisable to have a discussion about the incident (what happened, why, how to fix it, etc.). For some incidents, especially those concerning outages, a proper postmortem is a great idea.

You've likely participated in, or even perhaps led, a postmortem. Essentially, you get all interested parties together and discuss what went wrong, why, and how the team is going to make sure it doesn't happen again.

There's a nasty habit in postmortems that I've noticed: a blame culture. If you've ever been in a team where people were punished for mistakes or people felt compelled to cover up problem areas, you were probably in a blame culture.

If people fear retribution or shaming for mistakes, they will hide or downplay them. You can never fix deep, underlying issues if your actions after an incident are to blame a person.[2]

Wrap-Up

This jam-packed chapter covered a lot of material about your alerting, on-call, and incident management. To recap:

- Alerting is hard, but a few key tips will keep you on the right path:
  - Don't send alerts to email.
  - Write runbooks.
  - Not every alert can be boiled down to a simple threshold.
  - Always be reevaluating your alerts.
  - Use maintenance periods.
  - Attempt automated self-healing before alerting someone.
- Improving the on-call experience isn't too difficult with a few tweaks.
- Building a simplified and usable incident management process for your company should be prioritized.

Now that we've gotten alerting and on-call out of the way, let's move on to everyone's least favorite class from school: statistics!

---

2 A great book on this topic is *Beyond Blame* by Dave Zwieback (O'Reilly, 2015).

## CHAPTER 4

Statistics Primer

Statistics is an undervalued topic in the world of software engineering and systems administration. It's also misunderstood: many people I've spoken to over the years are operating on the misapprehension that "rubbing a little stats on it" will result in magic coming out the other end. Unfortunately, that isn't quite the case.

However, I am happy to say that a basic lesson in statistics is both straightforward and incredibly useful to your work in monitoring.

Before Statistics in Systems Operations

Before we get into the statistics lesson, it's helpful to understand a bit of the background story.

I fear that the prevalence and influence of Nagios has stifled the improvement of monitoring for many teams. Setting up an alert with Nagios is so simple, yet so often ineffective.[1]

If you want an alert on some metric with Nagios, you're effectively comparing the current value against another value you've already set as a warning or critical threshold. For example, let's say the returned value is *5* for the 15m load average. The check script is going to compare that value against the warning value or critical value, which might be *4* and *10*, respectively. In this situation, Nagios would fire an alert for the check breaching the warning value, which is expected. Unfortunately, it isn't very helpful.

---

1 I don't mean to pick on Nagios—it's just that Nagios, thanks to its influence, has set the expected standards in many tools. There are plenty of other tools just as guilty.

As so often happens, systems can behave in unexpected (but totally fine) ways. For example, what if the value crossed the threshold for only one occurrence? What if the next check, 60 seconds later, came back with a value of *3.9*? And the one after that was *4.1*? As you might imagine, things would get noisy.

Nagios and similar tools have built mechanisms to quiet the noise for this particular sort of problem in the form of *flapping detection*. This works simply and rather naively: the monitoring tool will silence a check that swings back and forth from OK to alerting too many times in a set time period. In my opinion, mechanisms like flap detection just cover for bad alerting. What if there were a better way?

Math to the Rescue!

One of the core principles of the modern monitoring stack is to not throw away the metrics the monitoring service gives you. In the old days, Nagios didn't record the values it received from a check, so you had no idea what trends were, whether last week or five minutes ago. Thankfully, it's commonplace to record this data in a time series database now, even with Nagios (see Graphios (*https://github.com/shawn-sterling/graphios*) and pnp4nagios (*https://docs.pnp4nagios.org/*)). Something often overlooked is that keeping data opens up many new possibilities for problem detection through the use of statistics.

Every major time series database in use supports basic statistics. The configuration and usage is different across each one, so I'm going to spend our time together in this chapter on the statistics themselves, rather than their use in a particular tool.

If you're used to the Nagios model of running checks, we'll need to change your thinking just slightly. Instead of having the monitoring system gather the data and check the values against a set threshold at the same time (typical Nagios behavior), let's decouple those into two separate functions.

We'll need something to collect the data and write it to the time series database at regular intervals (I'm a huge fan of collectd (*https://collectd.org/*) for this purpose). Separately, we'll have Nagios run its load average check not against the host directly, but against a metric stored in the time series database. You'll need to use a different check script for this, one that is built to query your TSDB of choice (see Nagios + Graphite (*https://github.com/pyr/check-graphite*), Sensu + Graphite (*https://github.com/sensu-plugins/sensu-plugins-graphite*)).

One of the new capabilities with this method is that you don't have to run the check against just the last reported value anymore—you can run it against a larger number of values. This will allow you to make use of basic arithmetic and statistical functions, leading you to more accurate problem detection. This additional amount of data is fundamental to everything in this chapter, as we can't tease out insights or predict the future without more of an idea of the past.

Statistics Isn't Magic

There seems to be a common feeling that if you "just rub some stats on it," you'll coax out some major insight. Unfortunately, this isn't the case. A lot of work in statistics is figuring out which approach will work best against your data without resulting in incorrect answers.

I cannot hope to do proper justice in this book to all the statistical methods you could possibly use—after all, volume upon volume has been written on the topic for centuries. Rather, I intend to teach you some fundamentals, dispel some misconceptions, and leave you in a position to know where to look next. With that, let's dive in.

Mean and Average

Mean, more commonly known as average (and technically known as the *arithmetic mean*), is useful for determining what a dataset generally looks like without examining every single entry in the set. Calculating the mean is easy: add all the numbers in the dataset together, then divide by the number of entries in the dataset.

A common use of averaging in time series is something called the *moving average*. Rather than taking the entirety of the dataset and calculating the average, it calculates the average as new datapoints arrive. A by-product of this process is that it *smooths* a spiky graph out. This process is also used in TSDBs for storing rolled-up data and in every time series graphing tool when viewing a large set of metrics.[2]

For example, if you had a metric with values every minute for the past hour, you would have 60 unique datapoints. As we can see from Figure 4-1, it's noisy and hard to see what's going on:

---

2 Loading several thousand datapoints from disk to display a graph takes a very long time, and you probably don't care about granularity when viewing four weeks' worth of data.

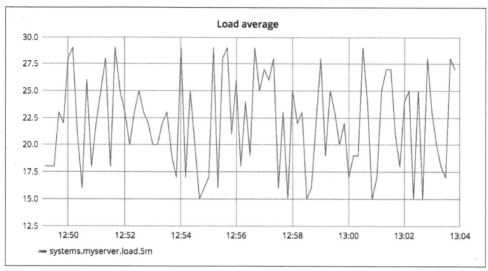

Figure 4-1. Load average

Applying a rolling average with five minute intervals yields a very different graph. This resulting graph shown in Figure 4-2 is what we call *smoothed.*:

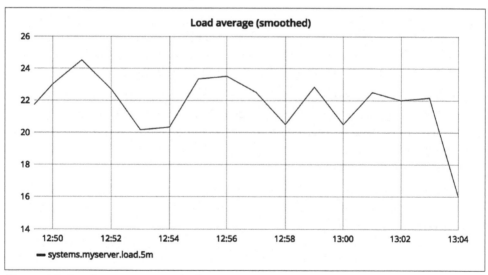

Figure 4-2. Load average, smoothed

That is, through the process of averaging values, the peaks and valleys have been lost. There are pros and cons to this: by hiding the extremes in the dataset, we create a dataset with patterns that are easier to spot, but we also lose datapoints that could be valuable. With more smoothing comes a better visualization at the expense of accuracy. In other words, determining the correct amount of smoothing to apply is a balancing act.

Median

Median is helpful when the average isn't going to be accurate. Essentially, the median is the "middle" of the dataset. In fact, median is often used for analyzing income levels of entire populations precisely for reason of accuracy. If you have 10 people, all with incomes of $30,000/yr, the average of their incomes is $30,000, while the median is also $30,000. If one of those 10 people were to strike it rich and have an income of $500,000/yr, the average becomes $77,000, but the median stays the same. In essence, when dealing with datasets that are highly skewed in one direction, the median can often be more representative of the dataset than the mean.

To calculate the median, you first must sort the dataset in ascending order, then calculate the middle using the formula $(n + 1) / 2$, where n is the number of entries in the dataset.[3] If your dataset contains an odd number of entries, the median is the exact middle entry. However, if your dataset contains an even number of entries, then the two middle numbers will be averaged, resulting in a median value that is not a number found in the original dataset.

For example, consider the dataset: *0, 1, 1, 2, 3, 5, 8, 13, 21*. The median is *3*. If we added a 10th number so the dataset becomes *0, 1, 1, 2, 3, 5, 8, 13, 21, 34*, then the median becomes *4*.

Seasonality

Seasonality of data is when your datapoints adopt a repeating pattern. For example, if you were to record your commute time every day for a month, you would notice that it has a certain pattern to it. It may not always be the same time each day, but the pattern holds day-to-day. You use this kind of knowledge every day to help you plan and predict the future: because you know how long your commute normally takes, you know when you need to leave in order to make it to the office on time. Without this seasonality, planning your day would be impossible. Figure 4-3 shows an example of seasonality in web server requests.

---

3 Your TSDB hides the underlying calculation from you, but trust me, this is what it's doing.

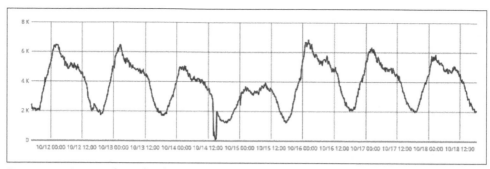

Figure 4-3. Seasonality of web server requests over seven days

If I know, based on previous data, that my web servers handle roughly 100 requests/sec on a given weekday, then I can also assume that half that number or double that number is maybe something worth investigating. Some tools allow you to apply this on a rolling basis, comparing datapoints now to datapoints at a previous time period, such as comparing req/sec currently to exactly the same time one week prior, one day prior, or even one hour prior. For workloads with a high degree of seasonality, you can thus make assumptions about what the future will look like. Not all workloads have seasonality—in fact, some have no discernible seasonality at all.

Quantiles

Quantiles are a statistical way of describing a specific point in a dataset. For example, the *50th quantile* is the mid-point in the data (also known as the median). One of the most common quantiles in operations is the *percentile*, which is a way of describing a point in the dataset in terms of percentages (from 0 to 100).

Percentiles are commonly found in metered bandwidth billing and latency reporting, but the calculation is the same for both. First, the dataset is sorted in ascending order, then the top *n* percent of values is removed. The next largest number is the *nth percentile*.[4] For example, bandwidth metering is often billed on a 95th percentile basis. To calculate that value, we would would drop the top 5% of values. We do this because it's expected in bandwidth metering that the usage will be bursty, so paying for bandwidth on a 95th percentile basis is more fair. Similarly, using percentiles for latency reporting gives you a good idea of what the majority of the experience is like, ignoring the outliers.

---

4 This is a rough definition and glosses over some subtleties of the underlying math. A more thorough treatment of percentiles can be found in "Statistics For Engineers" (*https://cacm.acm.org/magazines/2016/7/204029-statistics-for-engineers*) (Heinrich Hartmann, ACM Vol 59, No 7).

You Can't Average a Percentile

By the nature of calculating a percentile, you're dropping some amount of data. As a result, you can't average percentiles together because you're missing some of the data—the result will be inaccurate. In other words, calculating a daily 95th percentile and then averaging seven of those together does not give you an accurate weekly 95th^value. You'll need to calculate the weekly percentile based on the full set of weekly values.

While using percentiles will give you an idea of what most of the values are (e.g., in the case of latency, what most users experience), don't forget that you're leaving off a good number of datapoints. When using percentiles to judge latency, it can be helpful to calculate the max latency as well, to see what the worst-case scenario is for users.

Standard Deviation

The *standard deviation* is a method of describing how close or far values are from the mean. That sounds great at first, but there's a catch: while you can calculate it for any dataset, only a *normally distributed* dataset is going to yield the result you expect. Using standard deviation in a dataset that's not normally distributed may result in unexpected answers.

Distributions? Normal? Not-Normal?

A *distribution* is just a statistical term for describing a model of your dataset. Normal distributions look a lot like the graph. Not-normal distributions often have a *skew*, that is, the dataset may have multiple peaks, a long lead-in, a long tail, etc.

One handy bit about standard deviation is that the amount of data within specific deviations is predictable. As you can see from Figure 4-4, 68% of the data resides within one standard deviation of the mean, 95% within two standard deviations, and 99.7% within three standard deviations. Keep in mind that this holds true only for normally distributed datasets.

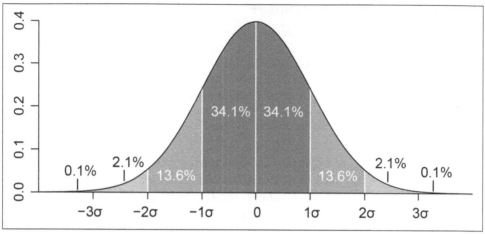

Figure 4-4. Normal distribution and standard deviation (Wikipedia, CC BY 2.5)

I mention standard deviation only because there's bad news: most of the data you'll be working with doesn't fit a model where standard deviation will work well. You're better off skipping right past using standard deviation rather than wasting time wondering why the calculation's results aren't what you were expecting.

Wrap-Up

This section has only barely scratched the surface when it comes to the world of statistics, but I've tried to focus on the most common and highest-impact approaches for operations and engineering work. To recap:

- Average is the most common and useful function you'll use, as it's widely applicable to lots of different datasets. Median is also quite handy, for some datasets.

- Seasonality is just a fancy way of talking about patterns in data based on time. Look at your traffic log and I bet you'll see seasonality.

- Percentiles are helpful for understanding what the bulk of your data looks like, but be careful: they inherently ignore the extreme datapoints.

- Standard deviation is a useful tool, but not so much for the sort of data you'll be dealing with.

I'll leave you with a few questions to consider when thinking about your data.

- Does it have a large skew in either direction? That is, do the datapoints cluster at either end of a graph?

- Are extreme outliers common?

- Are there upper and lower bounds for datapoints? For example, latency measurements can, in theory, be effectively infinite in the positive direction (bounded on the low end by zero), while CPU utilization percentage is bounded on both ends (0% and 100%).

By asking these questions of your data, you'll start to understand which statistical approaches may work well and which may not.

And with that, we've reached the end of Part I of *Practical Monitoring*! In Part II we'll get into the nitty-gritty of "What should I be monitoring? How do I do it?"

Monitoring Tactics

Part II of *Practical Monitoring* explores specific tactics of what to monitor and how. As you read through Part II, keep in mind the foundational principles you learned from Part I.

## CHAPTER 5

Monitoring the Business

If you recall from Chapter 2, we learned one of the important monitoring design patterns: monitor from the user's perspective. We learned that starting your monitoring efforts from the outside, rather than deep in the bowels of the infrastructure where most people start, is a far better approach as it provides you with immediate insight into the actual questions people are asking ("Is the site up?" "Are users impacted?") and sets the stage to iteratively go deeper.

The questions asked by business owners are often vastly different than those asked by software engineers or infrastructure engineers, and I think this is an area where we as engineers can improve our skills and understanding. Once we learn to ask the questions the executives are asking, we can really begin to work on the most important and highest-leverage problems facing the business.

In this chapter, you'll learn what those questions are and how to apply your engineering expertise to answering them while hitting the basics of business KPIs. By the end of the chapter, you'll have an appreciation for the concerns of executives and how you can make their lives easier while also demonstrating the value that monitoring provides to the business.

Business KPIs

A *key performance indicator* (KPI) is a metric that measures how your company is doing along lines the company has deemed important to the health of the business as a whole. A KPI, like a performance metric does for the app and infrastructure, tells you how your business is doing. Also like performance metrics, some metrics can be rather fuzzy about what they tell you and may require some degree of judgment in order to make decisions with them.

From an executive or founder's perspective, you can sum up their concerns fairly easily:

- Are customers able to use the app/service?
- Are we making money?
- Are we growing, shrinking, or stagnant?
- How profitable are we? Is profitability increasing, decreasing, or stagnant?
- Are our customers happy?

There are many metrics you can use to answer these questions, and they all tend to be approximations, requiring some level of judgment. After all, business is often messy —if it were easy, everyone would be doing it, right?

The following are common metrics business owners use to answer these questions:

Monthly recurring revenue
> Measures the amount of monthly recurring revenue from customers. Most often used by SaaS or managed services companies.

Revenue per customer
> Measures the amount of revenue per customer, generally on an annual basis. A good measurement for most types of companies.

Number of paying customers
> Self-explanatory. You probably want this number to be going up.

Net promoter score
> A measurement of user/customer satisfaction. *Net promoter score* (NPS) asks the user on a scale from 1 to 10, with 10 being the best (also known as a Likert scale), how likely they are to recommend the service/app to someone else. With enough responses, you can get a sense of how happy your users are with your service/ app. NPS can also be used at a more granular level, such as in follow up emails with recently resolved help desk tickets.

Customer lifetime value (LTV)
> The total value of a customer over their lifetime. If you are cross-selling to customers, this number should be going up. This measurement is closely related to revenue per customer but is measured on a lifetime basis.

Cost per customer
> Measures how much it costs to service a customer. You ideally want this number to be decreasing over time, as it means you are becoming more efficient at providing a service/app and therefore more profitable. If you are running a SaaS app, determining how much infrastructure costs to run per user is a good starting place for this metric.

Customer acquisition cost (CAC)

Measures how much it costs to acquire a customer/user. This is generally a metric that your marketing team lives and dies by.

Customer churn

Measure of how many users are leaving your app/service. Some amount of churn is inevitable and simply the nature of doing business, but high churn can indicate problems with the app, whether from a product perspective (your app just isn't very good), performance perspective (your app is too slow), or cost perspective (your app is too expensive). Churn rate is highly dependent on the nature of your business, so it's best compared to yourself over time and not to other businesses.

Active users

A measurement of active users for your app/service. Active users can be hard to define, and this measurement is greatly dependent on the nature of your business. This metric is often tracked as multiple metrics, such as *daily active users* (DAU), *weekly active users* (WAU), and *monthly active users* (MAU). Ideally, you want this number increasing.

Burn rate

A measurement of how much money the company is spending as a whole. This number includes everything from salaries to office space. If you're a revenue-generating company (e.g., later stage startup or enterprise), this number isn't generally used.

Run rate

Often found in conjunction with burn rate, run rate is a measurement of how long a company has before it's out of cash at current expenditure levels. This is usually expressed in months. If you're a revenue-generating company (e.g., later stage startup or enterprise), this number isn't generally used.

Total addressable market (TAM)

A measurement of how large a particular market is. It's fundamentally an estimate that is arrived at by determining the total dollar value if you were to sell to everyone in that market. This can fluctuate depending on how a company defines its market.

Gross profit margin

A measurement of profitability after cost of goods sold (COGS). If you're a SaaS company, this number is usually greater than 80% and often in the 90% range. COGS, for SaaS, is essentially what it costs to run the app/service. If you are a physical goods company, COGS is the cost to produce those goods. COGS does not include cost of salaries or office space. You can further divide this number by the number of users to determine how much it's currently costing you on a per-user basis.

Each of these metrics is used to answer different questions (or the same question from a different perspective!). It's sometimes hard to get this data, depending on the business. Given the sometimes sensitive nature of these metrics, you may not have access to the data yourself, but it's still important for you to understand what's being measured at the executive level and why. If you're interested in learning more about these topics, Andreessen Horowitz has two fantastic blog posts covering them.[1] Though they are aimed primarily at the startup world, they're a great starting point for digging in deeper on business-level metrics.

Two Real-World Examples

Since you're reading this book, you're probably in IT or engineering and now wondering what you can do about helping to monitor the business, and the answer is: a lot, actually!

If you're running a SaaS app, for example, there are a lot of questions that can be answered by instrumenting it. The examples that follow will show you exactly what I mean by monitoring from the outside first and why it's so helpful. Let's look at how a couple well-known companies might take this approach.[2]

Yelp

Yelp is an online platform that connects people with local businesses. There are two types of users for their platform: people searching for a local business (and possibly giving reviews) and business owners managing their business's page (and possibly giving responses to reviews). A business owner can "claim" their business page for free, but Yelp monetizes its platform by charging business owners for advertising.

Even from this small description, compiling a list of business KPIs is easily done:

- Searches performed
- Reviews placed
- User signups
- Business pages claimed
- Active users
- Active businesses
- Ads purchased

---

1 See *http://bit.ly/2yJOWRe* and *http://bit.ly/2zBRMo9*.

2 I'm making an educated guess here—I could be totally off base.

- Review responses placed

All of these measure core functionality of the Yelp app and, depending on the architecture, may have a strong or loose mapping to backend services. These metrics are great leading indicators that something might be going wrong somewhere for one simple reason: if the search functionality is broken or slower than normal, the number of searches performed is likely to drop. These metrics, over time, should be relatively stable. You'll get to know them at a glance and intuitively understand what looks right and what doesn't. Imagine if you had all these metrics on a TV in your office for all to see. Anyone walking by would be able to immediately get a sense of whether things were fine or going south. None of these metrics tell anyone what might be wrong, but they're great at signaling the overall health of the business.

Another side effect of tracking these metrics is that you'll be able to quickly see the impact of backend problems on users. How many times have you seen a slowdown in some backend service and wondered about the impact to users? If you've got these metrics, answering that question becomes as easy as popping open the dashboard.

Reddit

Reddit is a social networking site. Users can read Reddit without an account, but posting a thread, commenting, voting, or private messages requires an account. Reddit is monetized via ads and Reddit Gold, a premium-level account for users. Subreddits are unlimited and free to create, but also require an account.

Measuring the core functionality would probably look something like this:

- Users currently on the site
- User logins
- Comments posted
- Threads submitted
- Votes cast
- Private messages sent
- Gold purchased
- Ads purchased

Reddit's metrics aren't terribly different from Yelp's, are they?

By now, you're starting to get an idea of what you might be able to do for your company. On their own, these metrics aren't perfect, but they do measure interaction and engagement of users/customers. What would it look like if we kept going deeper with this line of thinking?

Tying Business KPIs to Technical Metrics

Let's go back to one of the examples above: Reddit. On its own, tracking user logins is good, but is there a way we could get more specific metrics about user login performance? I think there is: user login failures.

Tracking user logins would give you both successful and failed logins. That's not bad, but if the backend service responsible for handling user logins were having issues, this metric wouldn't show us. Tracking success and failure separately is even better, as it helps us in our ever-present quest to know whether our app is working.

Let's look again at Reddit's metrics, with a bit more granularity (Table 5-1):

Table 5-1. Business KPIs tied to technical metrics

Business KPI	Technical metrics
Users currently on the site	Users currently on the site
User logins	User login failures, login latency
Comments submitted	Comment submission failures, submission latency
Threads submitted	Thread submission failures, submission latency
Votes cast	Vote failures, vote latency
Private messages sent	Private message failures, submission latency
Gold purchased	Purchase failures, purchase latency
Ads purchased	Purchase failures, purchase latency

A couple things to note here:

- We've left current users alone. This metric is still very useful to us, as it provides clues about traffic levels to the site.
- The new metrics are all about failure rates and latency. You can track success rates if you'd like, but failure rates are more directly applicable to our goals. Latency is great to track, as it can be a good indicator of coming problems.

These new metrics answer the question of whether the app is working at a more granular level than the previous set did. They don't assume they know what the problem is, but only hint that there could be one—exactly where we want to be for these sorts of metrics.

My App Doesn't Have Those Metrics!

You might thinking about now, "My app doesn't give me that data. How do I monitor something I don't have?" I am so glad you asked.

Monitoring, as I mentioned in chapters 1 and 2, isn't something that can be bolted on after the fact. To get visibility into the performance of your app and infrastructure, you have to have a design for it.

Can you imagine if Ford made a car with no way to measure how much fuel was in the tank? Or how fast you were going? These aren't simply bolted onto the car after it's been finished—they were designed into the vehicle from the very start. In fact, modern vehicles are very much like modern software: the ECU (engine control unit, aka, "the computer") is just a whole lot of software responsible for analyzing inputs from lots of sensors and adjusting outputs given to the other components of the car. The core functionality of an ECU depends entirely on sensors feeding back measurements to it, allowing the ECU to adjust its controls of various critical components. Right from the beginning of the computerized era, monitoring was built into the vehicle at design.

Thankfully for us, we aren't building cars: we can change things whenever we like with a much faster feedback loop than, say, adding a gas gauge to every car we've sold after they've been shipped out. We have the ability to modify our apps and infrastructure to add better monitoring as we please and improve on it over time. If your app doesn't expose a measurement you need, get your hands dirty and modify the app to do so.

Finding Your Company's Business KPIs

Now that you've got an idea of how you can tie business KPIs to technical metrics, let's talk about how to find them for your business and app.

With the examples given, you've probably already got a decent idea of what your metrics are. I'd love to give you a list of metrics you should be tracking, but alas, every business is different, and sweeping generalizations can't be made.

However, don't fret, because I have a foolproof way of ensuring you understand how the app works and what's important to measure: talk to people.[3]

Yes, I know, it's crazy, but I swear it works!

So whom should you talk to?

The first person is a product manager. If you haven't worked with a product manager before, their job is to essentially understand what the customers want and work with engineering to get it built. As a result, product managers tend to have the best idea of what matters at a high level. After talking with product managers, talk to the man-

---

3 This is actually a mind hack of sorts: talking to people outside of Engineering gets you out of the engineering bubble, even if for a brief time. It's always valuable to understand perspectives outside of Engineering.

ager(s) of the software engineering team(s), followed by a few senior software engineers. By the end, you should have a great idea of what matters and how to find it.

What should you ask them? Here are my favorite questions:

- Let's assume I'm new to the company—how do I know the app is working? What do you check? How should it behave?
- What are the KPIs for our app? Why are those the KPIs? What do they tell us?

Another way to figure out what you should monitor at this stage is to sketch out the app's functionality at a very high level. Pay no attention to whether you're using MySQL or PostgreSQL or what-have-you for your database—simply knowing that some component talks to a database is sufficient to know that you probably want to measure database latency from that component. Mapping out functionality, such as login, search, loading a map, etc. is a great way to determine where to start.

Since every business is different, there are no common metrics everyone should track. Your goal is to find the high-level metrics that indicate whether the app is actually working as it should.

Wrap-Up

We've learned the importance of facets of the company that many of us are rarely, if ever, exposed to. Yet they are absolutely crucial to the operation and growth of the business—and us keeping our jobs. To recap:

- Business KPIs are among the most important metrics out there and make great leading indicators for the health and performance of your app and infrastructure.
- We learned how to identify these important metrics in our companies and track them.
- We learned how to tie business metrics to technical ones.

In the next chapter, we'll learn about the ever-evolving world of frontend performance monitoring.

## CHAPTER 6

Frontend Monitoring

Many companies often overlook frontend monitoring, usually due to monitoring being the "thing that Ops owns." Your average sysadmin/ops engineer doesn't often think about the frontend of an app, aside from the public-facing web servers. Unfortunately, this represents a pretty large blind spot, as we will soon see.

In this chapter, we'll talk about why this is a blind spot and how to change that by looking at various approaches for frontend monitoring. We'll wrap up the chapter with how to integrate frontend monitoring into other tools you're already using to make sure you don't lose those performance gains over time.

What do I mean by *frontend monitoring*? I define the frontend as all the things that are parsed and executed on the client side via a browser or native mobile app. When you load a web page, all of the HTML, CSS, JavaScript, and images constitute the frontend. All of the work a webapp does on fetching data from databases, executing backend code (e.g., Python, PHP), or calling APIs for data—that's the backend. As more and more work is moved from the backend apps to the frontend, this delineation can get a little blurry.

In fact, with the proliferation of *single-page apps* (SPAs), it's not uncommon for a spike in JavaScript errors to occur without any corresponding spikes in HTTP errors. Traditional approaches to monitoring simply aren't suited for a world of client-side browser apps.

What, Exactly, Is an SPA?

An SPA is a browser-loaded webapp where most, if not all, resources are loaded on the client side with few requests made to the server for data. One unique feature of many SPAs is that page refreshes are unnecessary, as the page updates its data in the background. React.js, Angular.js, Ember.js, and others are popular frameworks used for SPAs.

How you approach frontend performance is going to be a little different than what you're used to. Your goal with monitoring frontend performance isn't *stay up*, but rather, it's *load quickly*. Over time, as you develop new features in your app, frontend performance has a habit of taking a hit due to the size of *static assets*, that is, all of your images, JavaScript, and CSS.

Using the strategies here for assessing performance and ensuring your improvements aren't lost over time, we'll make sure your frontend performance is always improving —or, at least, you're always aware of where you stand.

Talking About Tools Without Talking About Tools

Monitoring the frontend (JavaScript) is hard to do from a generic, non-tool-specific position like we'll be doing in later chapters. Due to the way things are with Java-Script, everything is abstracted away and implemented as a particular library or tool. While I strive to be tool-agnostic in this book, doing so with JavaScript hasn't proven to be so easy. As a result, I'll mention a few specific tools and libraries in this chapter, but these should not be seen as endorsements, but merely examples.

The Cost of a Slow App

As engineers, we intuitively understand that a slow app is bad for business. I can't count how many times a day I get frustrated with a slow website and just move on. But how bad is it for the bottom line, really? How do you convey the importance of frontend performance in a tangible, dollars-focused way? How do you convince people that spending time on frontend performance is worthwhile? How do you measure the outcomes?

According to a 2010 study (*http://bit.ly/2y66Glp*) conducted by Aberdeen Research, a one-second delay in your page load time results in an average of 11% loss in page views, 7% loss in conversions, and 16% loss in customer satisfaction. Aberdeen found that the business begins to suffer when the page load time reaches 5.1 seconds, while the sweet spot for load time is under 2 seconds.

Shopzilla and Amazon had similar findings. Shopzilla's page load time dropped from 6 seconds to 1.2 seconds (*https://www.youtube.com/watch?v=Y5n2WtCXz48*), resulting in a 12% increase in revenue and a 25% increase in page views. Meanwhile, Amazon found (*http://bit.ly/2y494hq*) that revenue increased by 1% for every 100 ms of load time improvement.

In more recent times, Pinterest undertook a frontend performance project in March 2017 (*http://bit.ly/2iyxUio*) with equally astounding and impactful results: 40% drop in perceived wait time, 15% increase in SEO traffic, and a 15% increase in signups. As the authors of the blog post wrote, "Because the traffic and conversion rate increases are multiplicative, this was a huge win for us in terms of web and app signups." That's quite the endorsement for the impact of tuning for performance on the frontend.

What Should My Page Load Time Be?

Aim for under four seconds. It's a tough target to reach, but it's entirely doable. Don't believe you can? Amazon.com maintained roughly 2.4 seconds throughout the day of Amazon Prime Day 2017 (*http://bit.ly/2i3u7Wn*). That's under far more traffic than any of us are likely to experience, and they still did it.

Even with these hard, concrete numbers, it's amazing how many teams still don't prioritize frontend performance improvements. I was recently speaking with a colleague who specializes in this area and helps other companies get these same sorts of results. He observed that even though he could tie actual bottom-line dollar amounts to the improvement efforts, teams were still hesitant, and sometimes unwilling, to dedicate any time to the work. Don't be one of those teams: great site performance is a requirement for profitable businesses that sell something online.

Two Approaches to Frontend Monitoring

There are two main approaches to frontend monitoring: *real user monitoring (RUM)* and *synthetic*. The difference between them has to do with the type of traffic you're using for monitoring.

 Technically, these two approaches extend to all monitoring, not just frontend. You may know them as *whitebox monitoring* and *blackbox monitoring*.

If you've ever seen Google Analytics, that's a type of RUM. In essence, RUM uses actual user traffic for the monitoring data. It does this by having you put a small snippet of JavaScript on every page. When someone loads that page, it sends some metrics off to the monitoring service.

On the flip side, tools like WebpageTest.org are synthetic monitoring: they create fake requests under a variety of test conditions to generate the data. Many software vendors try to tout their RUM and synthetic monitoring tools as something unique and special, but the only thing special about them is their particular implementation.

RUM will be the core of your frontend monitoring efforts, as it's monitoring performance experienced by real users under real conditions. We're going to focus on methodology and foundations of RUM for much of this chapter, and wrap up with some thoughts on synthetic monitoring.

Document Object Model (DOM)

Before we get into the nitty-gritty of frontend monitoring, we first need to talk about a core concept: the *Document Object Model*, commonly known as the *DOM*.

The DOM is the logical representation of a web page. The DOM is roughly tree-like, with every HTML tag making up a *node* in the DOM. When a page is requested, the browser parses the DOM and renders it into a page that's visually readable. Technically speaking, HTML is not the DOM, nor is the DOM just HTML—though, to make things more confusing, a completely static website's source HTML is a complete representation of the DOM. As soon as you introduce JavaScript, the DOM and the HTML source diverge.

As you may know, a JavaScript script can reference an HTML element and change the data in it on the fly, after the page has loaded, making the page dynamic. If you've ever used an online calculator, you've seen this in action. This is how the modern web works, just with a whole lot more JavaScript and complexity. As a result of this capability, the DOM that the browser parsed and the final page your browser presented to you aren't the same.

The reason web page performance is a big deal is because of the multitude of ways JavaScript impacts it. By default, scripts are loaded synchronously. That is, if the DOM is being parsed and a <script> tag is encountered, the browser will stop parsing the DOM and load the script. This makes a full HTTP connection to request the script, download it, execute it, load it into the DOM, then continue with parsing the DOM.

HTML5 supports an async attribute on <script> tags, which tells the DOM to not block on loading the script. This async attribute allows the script to be downloaded in the background while the DOM continues to be loaded, executing the script when it's finished downloading. This capability improves page performance greatly, but it's certainly not a silver bullet.

I know this is a book about monitoring, so you might be wondering why we're talking about JavaScript so much. I find it's helpful to understand the underlying mechanics of what it is we're monitoring, and when it comes to frontend monitoring, we're really talking about the mess that JavaScript can cause.

To wit, imagine you have dozens of these scripts: you can see how page performance would degrade. As an example, as of this writing, *cnn.com* loads 55 scripts, while *google.com* loads a mere five. The load times correspond as you might imagine: 8.29 seconds for *cnn.com* and a snappy 0.89 seconds for *google.com*.

Frontend Performance Metrics

With that lesson about the DOM out of the way, let's get down to business: metrics. Many people aren't aware of how much data the browser itself collects and exposes to anything that asks for it. In fact, your browser exposes a wealth of information such as your device's battery level, current time, time zone, and even the size of your screen (and more!). Of course, we're interested in performance metrics, which the browser has as well.

While many of the tools available on the market abstract frontend measurements away, rolling them up into a nice easy-to-use package, it's helpful to understand what they're doing. In most cases, you're going to be using some SaaS tool to keep tabs on frontend performance, but let's look at what's going on under the hood.

Navigation Timing API

Browsers expose page performance metrics via the *Navigation Timing API* (*https://www.w3.org/TR/navigation-timing/*), a specification recommended by the W3C. This API is enabled by default for every page and provides a lot of information about the page performance. This API exposes 21 metrics in total, though in my experience, most of them are useful for troubleshooting performance while only a few are necessary for regular monitoring of trends.

The full list of metrics available in this API are shown in Table 6-1.

Table 6-1. Navigation Timing API metrics

navigationStart	unloadEventStart	unloadEventEnd
redirectStart	redirectEnd	fetchStart
domainLookupStart	domainLookupEnd	connectStart
connectEnd	secureConnectionStart	requestStart
responseStart	responseEnd	domLoading
domInteractive	domContentLoadedEventStart	domContentLoadedEventEnd
domComplete	loadEventStart	loadEventEnd

Figure 6-1 will make more sense of them:

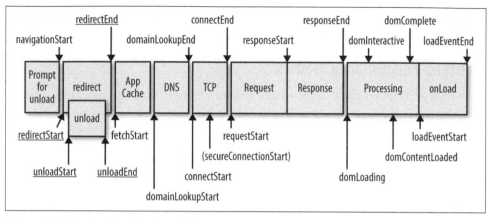

Figure 6-1. Navigation Timing API measurements

These are the metrics I've found most consistently useful:

- navigationStart
- domLoading
- domInteractive
- domContentLoaded
- domComplete

Let's look at what these mean in more detail:

navigationStart
This marks the time when the page request is made by the browser.

domLoading
This marks the time when the DOM has been compiled and begins loading.

domInteractive
This marks the time where the page is deemed to be usable, but not necessarily finished loading.

domContentLoaded
This marks the time when all scripts have been executed.

domComplete
This marks the time when the page has finished loading everything (HTML, CSS, and JavaScript).

There's another API in the browser called the *User Timing API* that's potentially useful for the more adventurous among you. Whereas the Navigation Timing API's metrics are set, the User Timing API allows you to create your metrics and events.

Speed Index

WebpageTest, being the de facto frontend performance testing tool, has quite a few interesting and useful metrics. Chief among them, one you may be familiar with already, is Speed Index (*http://bit.ly/1ttMTJ5*).

Whereas Navigation Timing metrics rely on accurate reporting by the browser, Speed Index uses video capture at a rate of 10 frames per second to determine exactly when a page is finished loading from a visual perspective. It's far more accurate than browser-reported metrics for determining the user-perceived completeness. The test results are then computed according to the Speed Index algorithm, which is represented as a single number where lower is better. Speed Index is a good number to get a general understanding of performance, but I would caution you about relying too much on it, since it doesn't include a lot of details that browser-reported metrics give you.

OK, That's Great, but How Do I Use This?

A list of metrics isn't that useful if you can't use them for anything. So, for example, with a little math, you can compute some useful numbers:

- `domComplete` - `navigationStart` = Total page load time
- `domInteractive` - `navigationStart` = Time until the user perceives the page as loaded

Once you're instrumenting your app to get this data, you can send it to any number of places. Example 6-1 shows how you can use Google Analytics and its `analytics.js` library to instrument your app, sending the metrics to Google Analytics:

Example 6-1. Using the Navigation Timing API with Google Analytics (code by Google)

```
// Feature detects Navigation Timing API support.
if (window.performance) {
  // Gets the number of milliseconds since page load
  // (and rounds the result since the value must be an integer).
  var timeSincePageLoad = Math.round(performance.now());

  // Sends the timing hit to Google Analytics.
  ga('send', 'timing', 'JS Dependencies', 'load', timeSincePageLoad);
}
```

If you'd prefer to use existing tools, such as StatsD and Graphite, you have a bit of a harder time. It's not straightforward to send to a UDP/TCP socket from JavaScript, but there are StatsD backends that accept an HTTP POST.

More likely (and I recommend this), if you're doing frontend monitoring, you'll be opting for a specialized SaaS product. These come with their proprietary libraries for instrumentation, and they're quite simple to use. Under the hood, they're leveraging the same APIs we've discussed, just in a very simple-to-use manner, plus great dashboards. If you're not going that route, the Google Analytics option is probably your best bet, especially if you're running a small site with little infrastructure.

Logging

If you've spent any time in the JavaScript world, you are likely already familiar with the `console` statement. `console` is used primarily for debugging and development purposes. For example: `console.log("This statement logs an entry");`. These sort of debug statements are certainly useful, but unfortunately, not all that helpful when you're wanting to stay on top of errors in production. After all, you don't want to be flooding the user's browser console with messages meant for you. For logging in production, you need something more robust.

Unfortunately, options are limited in this area. There's not much in the way of a generic logging infrastructure like `syslog`, resulting in dozens of libraries of varying quality that essentially try to accomplish the same goal of sending log entries somewhere.

However, if you can use a SaaS product, your options open up substantially: there are several products out there that handle all of the hard parts of collecting exceptions and log statements from JavaScript and sending them to a hosted service. Google for *exception tracking saas* and you'll find plenty of great options.

Synthetic Monitoring

If you've ever run `curl` on a website to ensure it was working, you've performed a synthetic test. There are tools out there that take it much further, specifically designed for web page performance. The big dog in that space is *WebpageTest.org*.

I've mentioned WebpageTest (they're the folks who created the *Speed Index*), but I want to come back to it for a particularly neat use case: integrating it into your testing suite. Performance of webapps tends to degrade over time, unless you actively optimize for performance on a regular basis. Since you can't improve what you don't measure, what if you could measure the frontend performance impact of every pull request? This is where WebpageTest private instances (*https://sites.google.com/a/ webpagetest.org/docs/private-instances*) save the day.

By making use of WebpageTest's API in your automated testing process, you can ensure your team is considering the performance impact of new features and not lose those hard-won performance gains.

Wrap-Up

As we've learned, frontend monitoring, despite being largely overlooked, is not only possible, but relatively easy to do. Like all monitoring, it's a rabbit hole that can go on seemingly forever, but the basics are simple:

- Monitor page load times for actual users.
- Monitor for JavaScript exceptions.
- Keep track of page load time over time with your CI system, ensuring load times stay within an acceptable range.

The frontend of your app is closely tied to the backend, though, and performance in the backend can often manifest as frontend issues (for example, slow reaction times when clicking buttons). To that end, let's move on to instrumenting the backend of your app (in other words, the code).

## CHAPTER 7

Application Monitoring

I've seen many companies with robust monitoring on their server infrastructure, great security monitoring, and a very capable network monitoring strategy—yet their applications are an unknowable black box. This always strikes me as odd, since most organizations are changing their applications more often than they are changing anything else, which means visibility into the performance of those applications should be of high importance.

I think it's mostly because many teams think application monitoring is too hard or requires some highly specialized skillset. Thankfully, neither is true, and this chapter will help you on your way to having high visibility into your applications.

Instrumenting Your Apps with Metrics

One of the most powerful things you can do in monitoring is also one of the most overlooked things: instrumenting your own applications. Why would you want to do this? Easy: your apps have a ton of valuable information about their performance, many of which will allow you to move from reactive to proactive in maintaining that performance.

One common fear I've heard is that it's difficult and time-consuming to add metrics to apps, but I'm here to tell you neither are true. As with all things, starting simple is the key: what about timing how long database queries take? Or how long some external vendor API takes to respond? Or how many logins happen throughout the day?

Once you start instrumenting your app, it becomes addictive. App metrics are so useful for a variety of things, you'll wonder why you didn't get started sooner.

An Aside About Application Performance Monitoring (APM) Tools

There are a lot of tools out there under the umbrella of *application performance monitoring* (APM) tools. The idea is that adding an agent or library to your app will allow them to automatically find all sorts of information about application performance, slow queries, and waterfall charts of your app. It's a compelling pitch, and it's not wrong: they will do all of these things and often more.

Here's the rub: these tools have zero context about your app or the business logic behind it. While you're looking at pretty waterfall charts of time spent on certain queries, it's not telling you anything about latency on a critical workflow path—or anything else that requires context around what it is the app does.

APM tools aren't bad, but understand their inherent limitations.

I know I've said that I wouldn't be talking about specific tools in this book, but there are exceptions. *StatsD* is one of those due to how easy it is to use in a variety of situations. It also perfectly illustrates how simple it is to instrument your apps.

StatsD is a tool used to add metrics inside of your code. Created by Etsy in 2011 (*http://bit.ly/2n7BmAo*), StatsD has become a staple in any modern monitoring stack due to its ease of use and flexibility. Even if you don't use StatsD, the takeaways are still valuable. StatsD was originally designed for a Graphite backend, so the metric names are dot-delimited (e.g., my.cool.metric).

I think explaining the value by example is the best way to really get a sense of the benefits here. Let's take this simple login function:

```
def login():
    if password_valid():
        render_template('welcome.html')
    else:
        render_template('login_failed.html', status=403)
```

If the password is valid, we return the welcome page (and an implicit HTTP 200), but if the login fails, we return the login_failed.html page and an HTTP 403 Access Denied. Wouldn't it be nice if we knew how often each happened? I'm so glad you asked:

```
import statsd
statsd_client = statsd.StatsClient('localhost', 8125)

def login():
    statsd_client.incr('app.login.attempts')
    if password_valid():
        statsd_client.incr('app.login.successes')
        render_template('welcome.html')
    else:
```

```
statsd_client.incr('app.login.failures')
render_template('login_failed.html', status=403)
```

I've added three metrics to this function now: how many times a login is attempted, how many logins succeed, and how many logins fail.

StatsD also supports timing how long something takes, and this is where we get into interesting things. What if our login service was a separate microservice, or even external? How would you know if things were about to go wrong?

```
import statsd
statsd_client = statsd.StatsClient('localhost', 8125)

def login():
    login_timer = statsd_client.timer('app.login.time')
    login_timer.start()
    if password_valid():
        render_template('welcome.html')
    else:
        render_template('login_failed.html', status=403)
    login_timer.stop()
    login_timer.send()
```

In this example, we're setting up a timer to record how long the function takes, in effect, telling us how long a login takes. Once you know how long it normally takes to process a login, the question of "Do logins seem slower to you?" is immediately answered with data instead of instinct and a shrug.

And that's only the beginning of what you can do with instrumenting your application with StatsD!

How It Works Under the Hood

StatsD is comprised of two components: the server and the client. The client is the code library itself that instruments the app and sends the metrics to the StatsD server over UDP. The StatsD server can live locally on each of your servers, or you can have a centralized StatsD—both patterns are commonly used.

The choice of UDP is important here. As UDP is a nonblocking protocol, that is, there is no TCP handshake to slow things down, instrumenting the app with StatsD calls won't have any significant impact on the app's performance. StatsD does support TCP as well, though I haven't found any good reason to use it over UDP.

StatsD "flushes" all collected metrics on its configured *flush interval* to all configured backends. By default, metrics are flushed every 10 seconds. An important bit about the flush is that all metrics collected during the flush interval are aggregated and then sent to the backend. Each data type aggregates in a different way.

Timers compute several separate metrics:

- The mean of the 90th percentile
- The upper bound of the 90th percentile
- The sum of the 90th percentile
- The upper bound of all timers in the time period
- The lower bound of all timers in the time period
- The sum of all timers in the time period
- The mean of all timers in the time period
- A count of the timers collected during the time period.

This sounds like a lot, but it's actually quite straightforward. For example, if you sent these values as timers:

```
5
9
30
25
7
3
2
15
17
80
```

then the results that StatsD would send are:

```
mean_90: 10.37
upper_90: 25
sum_90: 83
upper: 80
lower: 2
sum: 193
mean: 19.3
count: 10
```

If you send a gauge, only the last value in the flush period is sent. A set behaves the same way as a gauge. If you send a counter, then two metrics are sent: the counter value and the per-second value. For example, if you increment the counter 11 times during the flush period, then the counter value sent will be 11, and the per-second value will be 1,100 (*$value / ($flushInterval / 1,000)*).

On the backend, you can send metrics to all sorts of places, including Carbon (Graphite), OpenTSDB, InfluxDB, and many SaaS tools. Configuring a backend is different for each backend, but it's all straightforward. StatsD comes with the Graphite backend built in. Check the documentation for your specific backend on how to set it up.

There's a lot more to StatsD that you can find in the documentation, which I encourage you to read if you're interested. It's also worth mentioning that most of the SaaS monitoring vendors have their own implementation of StatsD or StatsD-like functionality.

Monitoring Build and Release Pipelines

Monitoring a build/release pipeline or procedure is an oft-overlooked aspect of the build-release process. Monitoring the process yields so much more insight and information into your app and infrastructure and helps you spot regressions and other problematic areas. You might be asking, "What could you possibly be monitoring here? A deploy either works or it doesn't!" That's mostly true. The real benefit here is in the meta-information (when did the deploy start, when did it end, what build deployed, who triggered the deploy) being available in the same place as your other app and infrastructure metrics.

Etsy popularized this concept in its seminal blog post, "Measure Anything, Measure Everything" (*http://bit.ly/2n7BmAo*), resulting in many different new ideas and tools for making it work even better. These days, most moderns metrics tools (both SaaS and on-premise) contain some way to implement this functionality (usually called *events*, *annotations*, or most aptly, *deployments*).

You're probably wondering why this is useful at all, so let's look at Figure 7-1: deployment events overlaid on API error rates.

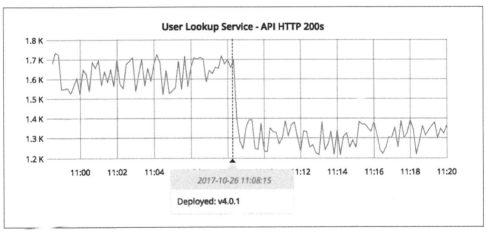

Figure 7-1. Deployment marker and API errors

The graph clearly shows a correlation between a recent deploy and significantly lowered API success rates. While correlation does not equal causation, this graph shows a strong case for the deploy having caused a problem somewhere. Recording information about deploy timing, the build data, and the deployer gives us more useful information for troubleshooting. Recording this information isn't often helpful by itself; but by combining this information with other metrics, we gain a whole new perspective and understanding of what our app and infrastructure is doing.

Health Endpoint Pattern

Oddly enough, this concept has been around for ages, but no one seems to have settled on an official name for the pattern. I've taken to calling it the */health endpoint pattern*, while there are also some articles online referencing the concept as a *canary endpoint*. Some just call it a *status endpoint*.

Whatever you call it, the concept is straightforward: an HTTP endpoint in your app that tells you the health of the app, and sometimes includes some basic information about the app (such as deployed version, status of dependencies, etc.). Underlying the endpoint is separate code that pulls information about the app's health and state. The implementation can range from simple to incredibly complex, as we'll soon see.

Why would you want to use this pattern? After all, we just spent several pages talking about how great push-based performance data is, so why would you want to use something that requires regularly pulling data?

There are several benefits to this pattern that you can't get with metric-based approaches:

- This endpoint can be used as the health check for a load balancer or for service discovery tools.
- The endpoint is helpful for debugging: exposing build information in the endpoint helps with determining what is running in the environment easily.
- Increasing the depth of the health check eventually yields an app that is aware of its own health.

Of course, it's not an either-or situation: you can implement both patterns, emitting metrics *and* providing a /health endpoint. Many teams do exactly that, depending on their needs.

Let's look at a simple implementation to illustrate. Consider a simple Django (a Python framework) app with a database dependency. I'm glossing over the underlying Django configuration, which I'm leaving as an exercise to you; this code is simply to illustrate how the health check might work, not how to use Django. You'll want to configure your app to call `health()` at whatever route you use (such as `/health`):

```
from django.db import connection as sql_connection
from django.http import JsonResponse


def health():
```

```
    try:
        # Connect to a SQL database and select one row
        with sql_connection.cursor() as cursor:
            cursor.execute('SELECT 1 FROM table_name')
            cursor.fetchone()
        return JsonResponse({'status': 200}, status=200)
    except Exception, e:
        return JsonResponse({'status': 503, 'error': e}, status=503)
```

This example reuses the existing database configuration for the app, which is a great idea so that you don't end up in the situation of the /health endpoint and the app using different credentials. This example just does a very simple query to return a single row. If the connection is successful, an HTTP 200 is returned, while an HTTP 503 is returned if it fails.

What if this app had more dependencies than just MySQL? What if it also depended on, say, Redis?

```
from django.db import connection as sql_connection
from django.http import JsonResponse
import redis


def check_sql():
    try:
        # Connect to a SQL database and select one row
        with sql_connection.cursor() as cursor:
            cursor.execute('SELECT 1 FROM table_name')
            cursor.fetchone()
        return {'okay': True}
    except Exception, e:
        return {'okay': False, 'error': e}


def check_redis():
    try:
        # Connect to a Redis database and retreive a key
        redis_connection = redis.StrictRedis()
        result = redis_connection.get('test-key')

        # Compare the key's value against a known value
        if result == 'some-value':
            return {'okay': True}
        else:
            return {'okay': False, 'error': 'Test value not found'}
    except Exception, e:
        return {'okay': False, 'error': e}


def health():
    if all(check_sql().get('okay'), check_redis().get('okay')):
        return JsonResponse({'status': 200}, status=200)
```

```
    else:
        return JsonResponse(
            {
                'mysql_okay': check_sql().get('okay'),
                'mysql_error': check_sql().get('error', None),
                'redis_okay': check_redis().get('okay'),
                'redis_error': check_redis().get('error', None)
            },
            status=503
        )
```

In this example, we've moved the two health checks into their own functions, then call them both from the health() function. If both return that they're working, the code returns an HTTP 200. However, if either one (or both) return otherwise, the code returns an HTTP 503.

If your service depends on other services, you could use this health check to check those too. For example, if your service has a hard dependency on an external API, why not check that?

```
from django.http import JsonResponse
import requests


def health():
    r = requests.get('https://api.somesite.com/status')
    if r.status_code == requests.codes.ok:
        return JsonResponse({'status': 200}, status=200)
    else:
        return JsonResponse({'status': 503, 'error': r.text}, status=503)
```

You aren't restricted to read-only operations with this, either—feel free to write data and test that. Let's see how that might look with our preceding Redis example:

```
from django.http import JsonResponse
import redis

redis_connection = redis.StrictRedis()


def write_data():
    try:
        # Connect to Redis and set a key/value pair
        redis_connection.set('test-key', 'some-value')
        return {'okay': True}
    except Exception, e:
        return {'okay': False, 'error': e}


def read_data():
    try:
        # Connect to Redis and retrieve the key/value we set
```

```
        result = redis_connection.get('test-key')
        if result == 'some-value':
            return {'okay': True}
        else:
            return {'okay': False, 'error': 'Redis data does not match'}
    except Exception, e:
        return {'okay': False, 'error': e}


def health():
    if not write_data().get('okay'):
        return JsonResponse({'status': 503, 'error': write_data().get('error')},
                            status=503)
    else:
        if read_data().get('okay'):
            # Clean up the old data before returning the HTTP responses
            redis_connection.delete('test-key')
            return JsonResponse({'status': 200}, status=200)
        else:
            # Clean up the old data before returning the HTTP responses
            redis_connection.delete('test-key')
            return JsonResponse(
                {
                    'status': 503,
                    'error': read_data.get('error')
                },
                status=503)
```

In this example, we first write a Redis key-value pair, then read the data back. If the value matches what we set (which means all connections worked well), then we return HTTP 200, and HTTP 503 if any part of the test fails.

As you can see, after only a few iterations of this pattern, the health check has become much more complex than when we first started. Using this pattern extensively in a distributed microservice architecture for every microservice would ultimately result in all your services knowing their own health at all times. Essentially, you would have just automated constant testing of the entire environment.

It is worth noting, however, that some teams have found that overly complex /health endpoints actually make it harder to debug problems when the endpoint says there's an issue, as well as the endpoint becoming needlessly noisy due to all of the dependencies it might be checking. It's not hard to imagine a scenario where a highly interconnected service has so many health checks that it would become hard to determine where problems actually lie.

One question people often have is whether the endpoint should be just another route in the app, or a separate app entirely. You want to do the former, so that your monitoring is shipped right alongside the app. Otherwise, you're defeating the point of this pattern.

One important thing I've found when using this pattern that is easy to overlook: you should be using the proper HTTP return codes. If everything is fine, return HTTP 200. If things aren't fine, return something other than HTTP 200 (HTTP 503 Service Unavailable is a good one to use here). Using the correct HTTP response codes makes it easy to determine when things are working, without having to parse any text that is returned.

Speaking of returning text, depending on what you're using this pattern for, it can be useful to return some data in the response. I'm a big fan of returning data as JSON, but feel free to use any other structured format—I don't recommend using unstructured formats, as they're more difficult to parse by machines. If your endpoint's implementation is relatively simple, then there's really no need to return data—just return an HTTP code and call it done.

What About Security?

I have heard objections to this pattern around security concerns. After all, you wouldn't want your users to be able to access this endpoint. You can generally solve this by using access restrictions on your web server and allowing only certain source addresses to access the endpoint, redirecting all others somewhere else.

There are downsides to this pattern, too. The biggest issue is that it's a lot more engineering work to implement than a simple metrics-based approach (that is, push-based) requires. You also need tooling that can consistently check the endpoint. If you come from metrics-based culture, you may not have this sort of infrastructure available to you.

So there you have it, the /health endpoint pattern. I'm rather fond of the pattern, but it certainly has its challenges and hurdles. In my opinion, the pattern is still useful, even if you aren't in a microservice environment, simply for being able to easily run a sanity check on the app.

Application Logging

Metrics can only tell you so much about what your application is up to, which is why it's important to also be logging behavior and actions from your applications.

If you recall back from Chapter 2, we talked about the importance of using structured logs over unstructured logs. While using structured logs in some server-side applications (e.g., Apache) requires real configuration that could be non-trivial for some people, emitting structured logs from your applications is super easy thanks to direct access to the data structures. Since JSON is simply a dictionary/hash, you can build up log data using those structures, then output using the logging library in your language of choice. Of course, many languages and frameworks have specialized libraries for emitting JSON-structured logs, which makes this even easier (to name a few, Python has `structlog`, Rails has `lograge`, and PHP has `monolog`).

Wait a Minute…Should I Have a Metric or a Log Entry?

The question of metric versus log can be a tricky one. Consider the following:

A metric: `app.login_latency_ms = 5`

A log entry: `{'app_name': 'foo', 'login_latency_ms': 5}`

If you have a sufficiently robust log analysis system, turning the log entry into metrics is trivial. A single log entry can contain significantly more metadata than a single metric entry can (in other words, more context):

```
{'app_name': 'foo', 'login_latency_ms': 5, 'username': 'mjulian', 'suc
cess': false, 'error': 'Incorrect password'}
```

This log entry is far more useful than the metric. In fact, from this log entry I can spot several distinct metrics that could be interesting. So why bother with metrics at all when logs can be so much more robust? Part of why this approach hasn't caught on is simply a matter of tooling: the tools that do support this sort of approach are still in their infancy (or very expensive). The other part is that the common wisdom just isn't there yet. My prediction: five years from now, we'll all be discussing better ways to do logging for the purpose of performance analysis.

Until then, I have two rules of thumb for log versus metric:

1. Is it easier for your team to think about metrics or logs?
2. Is it more effective for the thing in question to be a log entry or metric? (In other words, think through your use cases.)

What Should I Be Logging?

Anything and everything!

Well, that's not completely true. Writing logs for every little thing that happens is a great way to saturate your network or disk (depending on where you're writing the logs to) and could potentially create a bottleneck in the app, due to spending so much time on writing log entries. For a particularly busy app, this could be a very real concern: your app might spend more time writing log entries than it does on doing the work it was created for.

The Solution Is Log Levels…or Is It?

The concept of log levels has been around for quite some time. The *syslog* protocol has been around since the 1980s, though it was only codified 2001 in RFC 3164. A later RFC, RFC 5424, updated and codified a few more things, such as severity levels. If you've ever wondered where those severity levels DEBUG, INFO, ERROR, and others came from, that's where.

Many *NIX daemons support logging output based on these severity levels, getting more or less verbose depending on the level set. It's common that using DEBUG in production settings will make the service unusable, due to the volume of log entries being generated from the service.

Here's the problem with severity levels: you set them based on the assumption that everything is working fine. When you have a problem necessitating a DEBUG level (in other words, tricky, hard problems), you don't have the data you need in the logs (since you probably set the default severity level to INFO or ERROR). Now you're missing the data you desperately need.

When writing your own apps, you get to pick the severity level a particular entry is outputted at, which makes this problem much worse. Is an API connection failure severity ERROR? Or is it severity INFO? What if you have robust throttling, exponential backoff, retries, and other mitigation strategies? Are all of those DEBUG severity?

As you can see, severity levels are useful, but come with a big caveat. Use them wisely.

Instead of going wild and peppering logging statements everywhere, slow down a bit and think about the behavior of your application. When something goes wrong, what questions do you usually ask first? What information would be really useful to have during troubleshooting or even just for reporting mechanisms? Start there. In essence, it's impossible to set up logging (or any monitoring, really) for a system that you don't completely understand. Spend the time to think through the app, and the log statements you need (as well as metrics and alerts) will become obvious.

Write to Disk or Write to Network?

Write to disk, with a service that comes along at regular intervals to send to an external location.

Many log services support writing from inside the app directly to a network location. This makes it easy to ship your logs off for storage and analysis, but as your app's traffic increases, this could become a significant and troublesome bottleneck. After all, you're having to make a network connection every time you send a log entry, which can get expensive in terms of resource utilization.

Instead, it's better to write the log entry to a file on disk. You can have a service that comes along at regular intervals (even near real time) to send the log entries to an external location. This allows for log shipping to be done asynchronously from the app, potentially saving a lot of resources. You can have this done using `rsyslog`'s forwarding functionality. Alternatively, many of the SaaS logging services have agents that perform the same job.

Serverless / Function-as-a-Service

Consider this problem: a serverless app (which I'll refer to as a *function*) exists only as long as there is work to do. It's invoked, does a job, then ceases to exist. The entire execution time? Under a second. Sometimes way under.

How in the world do you monitor such a thing? Traditional polling models don't work: the polling interval isn't short enough.

Many serverless platforms are already recording some metrics for you, such as execution time, number of invocations, and error rates. But, you'd probably like to know about what's happening inside the function too.

The answer is quite simple: StatsD. Have a look back at the beginning of this chapter for more on that.

Also, don't forget: your functions are probably making use of other established services with metrics and logs already available (e.g., AWS S3, AWS SNS, etc.), so be sure to check on those too.

Of course, monitoring one or two functions is different from monitoring an entire architecture built around them. If you're in that situation, you are probably going to be very interested in distributed tracing. Let's take a look at that now.

Monitoring Microservice Architectures

In a world where microservices are taking over everything, great monitoring becomes a must-have. Whether you've got three or four microservices or a hundred (or more!), understanding the interactions between these services can get complex, which makes monitoring challenging.

Consider the case of the monolith application in Figure 7-2:

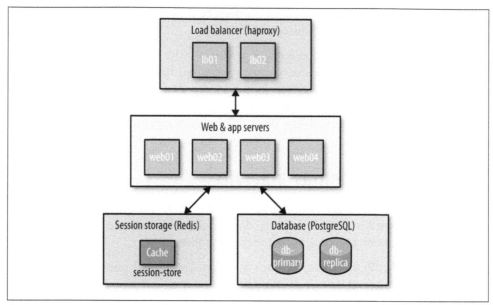

Figure 7-2. A simple monolith app architecture

It's easy and straightforward to understand the requests coming in, the results going out, and what's happening between. And remember, a monolith need not be run on a single server—this example shows a monolith application scaled horizontally across four nodes.

What happens if we have even a small microservice environment? Imagine the preceding architecture—except repeated multiple times and abstracted away as a standalone service. Suddenly, you're no longer certain where a request started, where it ended up, and where it might have gone wrong (Figure 7-3). Latencies are hidden in a microservice architecture unless you have rather robust and mature monitoring practices.

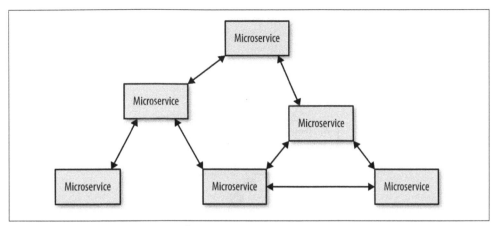

Figure 7-3. Microservice app architecture

Suddenly, understanding what happens with user requests is much more challenging. Enter distributed tracing.

Distributed tracing is a methodology and toolchain for monitoring the complex interactions inherent in a microservice architecture. Popularized by the Google Dapper paper and first implemented outside of Google with Zipkin, distributed tracing is becoming an integral component of the monitoring toolset for teams running microservice architectures.

How it works is straightforward: for every request that comes in, "tag" it with a unique request ID. This request ID stays with the request and resulting requests throughout its life, allowing you to see what services a request touches and how much time is spent in each service. One important distinction of tracing versus metrics is that tracing is more concerned with individual requests than the aggregate (though it can also be used for that). Figure 7-4 shows an example of a trace.

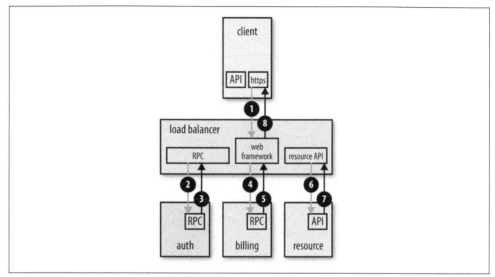

Figure 7-4. An example trace[1]

Distributed tracing is far-and-away the most challenging and time-consuming monitoring technique to implement properly, not to mention only being useful for a small segment of the industry. Distributed tracing is not for the faint of heart or the understaffed-and-overworked engineering team. If you've already got all the metrics and logs you want, but still find yourself struggling to understand inter-service performance and troubleshooting in a distributed architecture, then distributed tracing might be for you (and the same goes for those of you with significant serverless infrastructures). Otherwise, effectively instrumenting your apps with metrics and logs is going to result in much better (and quicker!) outcomes.[2]

---

1 Based on an example trace found in the OpenTracing Framework documentation (*http://opentracing.io/docu mentation/*); Copyright OpenTracing Project.

2 That said, tracing tools are consistently improving in their implementation complexity. I suspect in a couple of years my warning will be moot.

Wrap-Up

To summarize what we've learned in this chapter on application monitoring:

- Instrumenting your application with metrics and logs is one of the most impactful things you can do for increasing your ability to understand and troubleshoot the performance of your applications.
- Tracking releases and correlating with performance in your apps and infrastructure.
- The /health endpoint pattern is pretty neat, though really only useful for certain architectural designs.
- Serverless and microservice monitoring really isn't that different from any other application, unless you have a sizable deployment. Then distributed tracing is probably where you want to begin investing time and effort.

Application code runs on servers somewhere, of course, and the performance of those servers has huge impact on the performance of your application. Let's go look at what it means to monitor your server infrastructure.

## CHAPTER 8

Server Monitoring

With many monitoring efforts beginning in the sysadmin/ops engineer team, it's no wonder that many of us immediately associate "monitoring" with "the thing the sysadmins do." This is unfortunate since we've seen there's so much more to monitoring than just what happens on a server.

Of course, there's an element of truth in the misconception: a lot *really does* happen on the server! Even in a serverless architecture, there are still servers underneath that provide the platform and all that makes it tick. We're going to delve down into what sort of common services you'll encounter on servers these days, what metrics and logs are provided, and how to make sense of it all.

One note before we jump in: this chapter is going to use Linux as the assumed operating system, since that's what I'm most familiar with. For the readers applying these lessons to Windows, nearly all of the stuff we'll be covering is just as applicable to Windows in a general sense, though your tools are different.

Standard OS Metrics

Over the course of this book, I've railed against the obsession with the standard OS metrics (CPU, memory, load, network, disk) and for good reason: starting your monitoring work with them is starting with the metrics that offer the least signal of all toward your main concern (that your app is working). In order to know if things are working, you have to start at the top instead, which I covered xref.

However, that isn't to say these metrics are not without usefulness. In fact, they can be an ally when used in the proper context: diagnostics and troubleshooting. In that context, these metrics are some of the most powerful metrics you have available.

My recommendation for how to use these metrics: automatically record them for every system you have, but don't set up alerts on them (unless you have a good reason). Pretty much every monitoring tool out there collects these by default with little to no intervention from you; so rather than discuss how to collect them, I'm going to discuss what they mean and how to use them. I'll be using well-known Linux command-line tools in my explanations—tools that you are likely well-acquainted with.

CPU

Monitoring CPU usage is the most straightforward of all these metrics. The metrics come from */proc/stat* and are available interactively with a number of utilities. We'll use top here:

```
top - 21:13:27 up 98 days,  2:01,  1 user,  load average: 0.00, 0.01, 0.05
Tasks: 105 total,   1 running, 104 sleeping,   0 stopped,   0 zombie
%Cpu(s):  0.0 us,  0.0 sy,  0.0 ni,100.0 id,  0.0 wa,  0.0 hi,  0.0 si,  0.0 st
KiB Mem:    500244 total,   465708 used,    34536 free,    85104 buffers
KiB Swap:        0 total,        0 used,        0 free.   244488 cached Mem
```

The third line has the CPU information we want: the percent utilization. As we can see, this particular server is 100% idle (id). To determine the utilization percentage, add user (us), system (sy), niced processes (ni), hardware interrupts (hi), and software interrupts (si). iowait processes (wa) and stolen time (st) aren't included, since they are waiting rather than being serviced.

Memory

Percent used versus free is the main thing here. Memory used can be further broken down by shared, cached, and buffered, which are all counted as "used." Most tools report memory metrics based on values reported by */proc/meminfo*. Here we'll use the free command, which gets its data from */proc/meminfo* as well, with the -m switch to show megabytes to make this discussion easier on us both:

```
                  total      used      free    shared   buffers    cached
Mem:                488       426        62        31        75       222
-/+ buffers/cache:            127       360
Swap:                 0         0         0
```

The output is often misunderstood, so let's break it down. The first row would seem to say that this system has 488 MB of total memory, 426 MB used, and thus 62 MB free, but what's with the remaining columns? And row two?

First, let's talk about *buffers* and *caches*. In Linux memory management, file system metadata (such as permissions and contents of a directory) for recently accessed areas of the disk are stored in buffers. The expectation is that you're likely to request this information again soon, so storing it in buffers will result in a quicker access time for you. Caches work similarly but for the contents of recently accessed files. Being that these are transient areas of memory with oft-changing contents, the memory used by them is technically available for use by any processes that need the memory.

Now, about that second row: since the memory is available should it be required, the second row is more useful for determining memory usage. This row represents memory used (minus buffers and cache) and free (plus buffers and cache). When determining whether you need more memory on a system, look at the second row, not the first. Some tools record memory used/free with buffers and cache built into the calculation, while some report the straight metrics from */proc/meminfo*, leaving you, the user, to do the math on what the memory usage really is.

The third line is self-explanatory: swap. If your systems use swap partitions/files (they're relatively uncommon in cloud infrastructure these days), then track it. Alerting on low free memory and increasing swap utilization is a great indicator of increased memory pressure, if your app is memory-sensitive.

Another way to watch for serious memory issues is by monitoring the *OOMKiller* spawning in your logs. This process is responsible for terminating processes in an effort to increase the available memory to a system when it's under high pressure. Grepping for `killed process` in your syslog will spot this. I recommend creating an alert in your log management system for any occurrences of OOMKiller. Any time the OOMKiller is coming into the picture, you've got a problem somewhere, especially because OOMKiller is unpredictable in its choice of target processes to terminate.

Network

Monitoring network performance on a server is similar to the network: all the same metrics apply. The information ultimately comes from */proc/net/dev* on Linux with both *ifconfig* and *ip* (from the *iproute2* package) being the de facto tools for interacting with it. At minimum, be sure to collect octets in/out, errors, and drops on your server interfaces. For details on what these metrics mean, reference Chapter 9.

Disk

Disk performance can be viewed in a variety of ways interactively, but they all read from the same source: */proc/diskstats*. We'll use *iostat* (available in the *sysstat* package, along with many other great tools) with the *-x* flag to give us an extended set of metrics to look at:

```
~$ iostat -x
Linux 3.13.0-74-generic (ip-10-0-1-196) 12/03/2016 _x86_64_ (1 CPU)

avg-cpu:  %user   %nice %system %iowait  %steal   %idle
          0.09    0.01    0.01    0.03    0.00    99.86
```

```
Device:         rrqm/s  wrqm/s    r/s    w/s   rkB/s    wkB/s avgrq-sz
xvda              0.00    0.21   0.06   0.40    1.53     3.64   22.41

                avgqu-sz  await r_await w_await  svctm  %util
                    0.00   1.16    0.89    1.21   0.34   0.02
```

We can see that I only have one disk and that it's mostly idle. *iowait* is an important metric here: it represents the amount of time the CPU was idle due to waiting on the disk to complete operations. High iowait is something we want to avoid.

The bottom part of the *iostat* output talks specifically about our disk performance. There are a bunch of metrics here, some more useful than others. In the interest of brevity, I'm only going to hit the most important ones: *await* and *%util*. These two metrics directly speak to the utilization and pressure on the disk.

await is the average time (in milliseconds) taken for issued requests to be served by the disk. This number includes both the time spent in queue and the time spent performing the request. *%util* is most easily thought of as the level of usage saturation of the disk. You'll want to keep this under 100%. Do note, however, that this metric can be misleading when the volume in question is part of a RAID array due to an inability to inspect it on a per-disk basis.

Running `iostat` without -x gives us another very useful metric: tps. +tps=, or transfers per second, is also known as *I/O per Second* (IOPS). IOPS is an important metric for any service that makes use of disks, such as database servers:

```
~$ iostat
Linux 3.13.0-74-generic (ip-10-0-1-196) 12/03/2016 _x86_64_ (1 CPU)

avg-cpu:  %user   %nice %system %iowait  %steal   %idle
           0.09    0.01    0.01    0.03    0.00   99.86

Device:            tps   kB_read/s    kB_wrtn/s    kB_read    kB_wrtn
xvda              0.46        1.53         3.64   12987412   30858420
```

IOPS is a useful metric for determining when you need additional transfer capability (e.g., more spindles) or for spotting general performance issues. For example, if you're tracking IOPS over time and you notice that this metric has experienced a sudden drop, you may have a disk performance problem on your hands.

Load

Load is a measurement of how many processes are waiting to be served by the CPU.[1] It's represented by three numbers: a 1 m average, a 5 m average, and a 15 m average.

---

1 For an extended look at load averages, Brendan Gregg wrote a great article (*http://bit.ly/2z5WM89*) on the topic.

The most common method to see this interactively is via the *uptime* command (which pulls data from */proc/loadavg*):

```
~$ uptime
 19:41:21 up 98 days, 29 min,  1 user,  load average: 0.00, 0.01, 0.05
```

A system with one CPU core and a load of 1.0 means that there is exactly one process waiting. Generally speaking, a load of 1.0 per core is considered to be perfectly acceptable.

The problem is that the load metric doesn't translate to system performance. It's not uncommon to find a server with a high load metric that is performing just fine. I've seen web servers with a 15 m load metric of over 500, but customers still able to use the system with no impact. As we learned back in Chapter 1, if nothing is impacted, is there really a problem?

The one exception to this is that load makes for a somewhat decent *proxy metric*. That is, an abnormal load metric is often an indicator of other problems (though, sometimes it isn't!).

In general, I think relying on the load metric for anything is a waste of time.

SSL Certificates

I'm sure every person reading this book has had an SSL certificate expire on them without realizing it until it was too late. It sucks, but it happens.

Monitoring SSL certificates is simple: you just want to know how long you have until they expire and for something to let you know before that happens.

There are a few options I've found for how to best handle this problem:

- Many domain registrars and certificate authorities (CAs) are capable of monitoring and alerting you on SSL certificate expiration (if you bought the certificate through them). This is the easiest method to implement. The downside is that they often alert you via email, which as we know, means you'll probably miss it. Another downside of this is that you're only checking the certificate itself, not the location where the certificate is in use, which is especially problematic for a wildcard certificate that might be installed in a dozen locations. If the alert can only come in via email, I recommend having it sent to a ticket system so you get a ticket opened instead of sitting in someone's inbox.

- If the SSL certificate is in use externally, you can use external site monitoring tools (e.g., Pingdom and StatusCake) to check and alert you on the certificate expiration. Tools such as these have the flexibility we want, but the downside is that they can't monitor anything that isn't publicly accessible (such as an internal service).

- If you have a lot of internally used SSL certificates, you're left with one option: an internal monitoring tool of some sort to check and report on the certificate. I haven't found any great tools for this, but a simple shell script that runs regularly and reports to your monitoring system or ticket system works rather well. Many on-premise monitoring systems also have the ability to monitor certification expiration.

SNMP

Let me put this in no uncertain terms: stop using SNMP for servers.

I'll be going into much more detail about how SNMP works and the challenges of working with it in Chapter 9, but suffice it to say: it's not a fun protocol to work with. Though you're (mostly) stuck with it for the purpose of monitoring network gear, that's (thankfully) not the case when it comes to monitoring servers.

Why shouldn't you use SNMP?

- Adding more functionality means extending the agent, which is a pain.
- It requires running an inherently insecure protocol on your network. Yes, there is v3, which has encryption and some semblance of a security model, but it's nowhere near enough. Your security folks will thank you for not doing this.
- It requires a centralized poller for gathering metrics, which can be difficult to scale and manage. This isn't a deal-breaker, as there are certainly ways to make this no longer a problem (some modern monitoring tools use centralized pollers).
- There are far better options available with easier configuration and more capabilities.

Rather than using SNMP, opt for a push-based tool like collectd (*https://collectd.org/*), Telegraf (*https://github.com/influxdata/telegraf*), or Diamond (*https://github.com/python-diamond/Diamond*).

Web Servers

If you're in the enterprise world, your experience with web server performance is likely limited to low-traffic, single-node web servers. However, if you're in the webapp world, the performance of your web servers are one of the most critical components of your app. Monitoring web servers doesn't differ between the two use cases, though the amount of time you spend looking at the metrics will obviously be higher for those in the webapp world.

When it comes to web servers, there is one golden metric for assessing performance and traffic level: *requests per second* (req/sec). Fundamentally, req/sec is a measurement of throughput. Less critical to performance, but still important for overall visibility, is monitoring your HTTP response codes. As you may know, the HTTP protocol has many different possible responses to a request. The most common is 200 OK, while there are also other common ones, such as 404 Not Found, 500 Internal Server Error, and 503 Service Unavailable.

Table 8-1. HTTP response codes (abbreviated)

Response code group	Group meaning	Common response codes
1xx	Informational	100 Continue
2xx	Success	200 OK, 204 No Content
3xx	Redirection	301 Moved Permanently, 302 Found
4xx	Client errors	400 Bad Request, 401 Unauthorized, 404 Not Found
5xx	Server errors	500 Internal Server Error, 503 Service Unavailable

In total, there are 61 official HTTP responses (*http://bit.ly/2z5xwz3*), though some applications and web servers implement additional ones.[2]

These response codes are recorded in the request log for your web server. For example, on NGINX, an entry looks like this:

```
10.0.1.52 - - [10/Dec/2016:19:41:17 +0000] "GET / HTTP/1.1" 200 24952
"http://practicalmonitoring.com/" "Mozilla/5.0 (Windows NT 6.2; WOW64)
AppleWebKit/537.4 (KHTML, like Gecko) Chrome/98 Safari/537.4"
"192.168.1.50"
```

Between the request command (GET / HTTP/1.1) and the byte size of the request (24952) is the HTTP response—an HTTP 200 in this case, showing that the request was successful.

Of course, not all requests are successful. A rising number of non-200 responses (such as 5xx or 4xx) to clients can indicate issues with your app which could be costing you real money in lost sales.

There's another metric that often gets people confused: connections. The short answer here is that connections are not requests, and you should pay more attention to requests than to connections. The longer answer leads us to the topic of *keepalives*.

Prior to the use of keepalives, each request required its own connection. Given that websites have multiple objects that need to be requested for the page to load, this led

---

2 For the full list of defined HTTP responses, see RFC 7231 Section 6 (*http://bit.ly/2z5xwz3*).

to a whole lot of connections. The trouble is that opening a connection requires going through the full TCP handshake, setting up a connection, moving data, and tearing down the connection—dozens of times for a single page. Thus, HTTP keepalives were born: the web server holds open the connection for a client rather than tearing it down, to allow connection reuse for the client. As a result, many requests can be made over a single connection. Of course, the connection can't be held open forever, so keepalives are governed by a timeout (15 seconds in Apache, 75 seconds in NGINX). There is also keepalive configuration on the browser side called *persistent connections* with their own timeout values. All modern browsers use persistent connections by default.

One final useful metric is request time. NGINX (*http://bit.ly/2y35qnY*) and Apache (*http://bit.ly/2gJ76vc*) both expose request time on a per-request basis in the access logs. By default, this isn't included, so you'll need to update the log format to include it.

Database Servers

The first thing to monitor is the number of connections. Of particular note here is MySQL: for reasons beyond the scope of this book, MySQL refers to its client connections as *threads*, spawning exactly one thread per client connection, so don't be confused when you go looking for the connections metric and can't find it. All the other database engines refer to them as simply *connections*.

While the number of connections to your database is a good indicator of overall traffic levels, it isn't necessarily indicative of how busy the database actually is. For that, we'll need to look at *queries per second* (qps).

Measuring queries per second is a much more direct measurement of how busy a server is. The qps measurement will fluctuate more in sync with actual busyness of the app and is a wonderful indicator of exactly how loaded your database servers are.

Slow queries are the bane of high-performance database infrastructures. A slow query will often manifest as a slow user experience, which we certainly don't want. There are lots of reasons for slow queries and many strategies for fixing them, but \ the first step to fixing slow queries is finding them. Slow queries are logged in a log file with the execution time, number of times executed, and the exact query. There are many tools out there that make parsing this information easier (usually APM tools).

If you're running a database infrastructure of any scale, you're probably using replicas (previously known as *slaves*, but many vendors have changed the terminology) so monitoring replication delay is important—you certainly don't want to find out about an out-of-sync replica days later. A normal delay is determined by the settings in your database server's configuration.

Finally, of particular importance here is the IOPS measurement I introduced at the start of this chapter. Databases are generally IO-constrained due to being heavy on reads/writes, so make sure you keep tabs on IOPS. Nothing is more frustrating than troubleshooting slow database performance and finding out an hour into it that it's just a failing disk that's caused IOPS to drop.

Entire books could be written about database performance monitoring and tuning. Oh wait, they have! I highly recommend reading Baron Schwartz's *High Performance MySQL* (O'Reilly, 2008) and Laine Campbell and Charity Majors' *Database Reliability Engineering* (O'Reilly, 2017). If you're at all interested in squeezing the most out of your database infrastructure and building for scalability, definitely read those.

Load Balancers

Load balancers are most often used for HTTP traffic, though they can be used for other types of traffic. We're only going to talk about HTTP here, though.

Load balancer metrics are very similar to web server metrics in that you're tracking the same sorts of things. Load balancers function by presenting themselves to the client as a single node. There may be any number of servers on the backend that the remote client never interacts with directly. As such, the metrics are duplicated in two groups: *frontend* and *backend*. It's the same set of metrics, but they tell you different things about the health of the load balancer itself and the backend servers. You'll want to pay attention to both sides.

It's worth mentioning here again that load balancers determine the state of their backend servers through a health check. The simplest health check is a simple connection to a specific port (such as checking that port 80 responds), but many load balancers also support HTTP health checks, which makes the /health endpoint pattern from Chapter 7 quite useful in load balancer health checks.

Message Queues

A message queue is made up of two "speakers": a *publisher* and a *subscriber* (message queues are sometimes called pub-sub systems because of this). Monitoring a queue is primarily about two things: *queue length* and *consumption rate*.

Queue length refers to the number of messages on a queue waiting to be taken off by one or more subscribers. A normal queue length depends on how your app works, so you want to pay attention to queues that get backed up with more messages than normal. *Consumption rate* is the rate at which messages are being taken off of the queue, or consumed. This metric is usually expressed in messages per second. Just as with queue length, a normal consumption rate depends on how your app works. Watch for an abnormal rate.

Any messaging queue software is going to provide you with significantly more metrics than just those two, and you'll want to determine if they're useful for your environment or not by reading the relevant documentation. Start with these two though, and you'll be good for a while.

Caching

A cache's primary metrics are the number of *evicted items* and the *hit/miss ratio* (sometimes called the *cache-hit ratio*).

As the cache grows, older items are removed from the cache—evicted, that is. High evictions are a good signal for a cache being too small, causing too many items to be evicted in order to make room for new items.

When your app requests something from the cache and the item is found, it's referred to as a *cache hit*. Likewise, if the item is requested and not found, it's called a *cache miss*. Given that the purpose of a cache is to speed up common requests, cache misses slow things back down. Therefore, watching the hit/miss ratio is a great indicator of cache performance. Ideally, you'd want this at 100% hit, but that's usually unrealistic for modern apps. Over time you'll start to understand what a normal ratio is for your app.

These metrics are closely related and work together—it's a balancing act.

DNS

Unless you're running your own DNS servers, there's really nothing to monitor here. In case you are running your own DNS servers, well, that's a different story.

If you're running your own DNS, there are a few things you're going to care about: *zone transfers* and *queries per second*.

Without going too deep into the inner workings of DNS, slaves are kept in sync with the master via zone transfers. Depending on configuration, these can be either transfer of the full zone (AXFR) or incremental transfers (IXFR). These are recorded in the log, and you'll want to keep tabs on them for spotting sync issues. An out-of-sync slave will serve up potentially stale information, which is going to leave you with odd troubleshooting problems.

Monitoring queries per second helps you to understand the load your servers are facing and are the primary measure of it for DNS servers. You'll want to record it on at least a per-server basis, but per-zone and per-view is much better for more granularity in your metrics.

If you are running BIND, check out the *statistics-channel* (*http://bit.ly/2yN3JcM*) configuration option: enabling it will expose all of these metrics in one place. Many tools are out there to take advantage of this, such as collectd's BIND plugin.

NTP

Some of the weirdest issues I've ever troubleshot have come down to poor time synchronization. For example, Kerberos tickets (authentication system used in Linux and Microsoft's Active Directory) are strongly dependent on accurate time synchronization between servers and clients. Some apps also make use of the system time for kicking off jobs, while accurate time is a crucial aspect of troubleshooting a distributed architecture.

The NTP system can be complex and esoteric, but if you're only running clients and not your own stratum 1 server, then there's only one thing you need to be concerned with: time drift between the client and server.

ntpstat, available in Ubuntu 15.10 and later and CentOS 7 and later, is useful for giving you a quick answer to whether a client is synced properly or not:

```
~$ ntpstat
unsynchronised
    polling server every 64 s
```

And when it's in sync:

```
~$ ntpstat
synchronised to NTP server (96.244.96.19) at stratum 3
    time correct to within 7973 ms
    polling server every 64 s
```

What's neat is that the exit code from ntpstat corresponds to whether it's synced or not, making for an easier way to monitor it: 0 for synced and 1 for unsynced. Using a shell script or something more advanced (such as collectd) makes monitoring this straightforward.

There are plenty more metrics you can look at if you're running NTP servers yourself, but this is becoming uncommon. If you do run NTP servers, you'll need to pay attention to drift between peers and your servers as well (ntpdate provides this information).

Miscellaneous Corporate Infrastructure

For those of you running traditional corporate infrastructure, there are two more things you might be managing that those in web-based environments won't be contending with: DHCP and SMTP.

DHCP

There are two things you want to pay attention to here: the DHCP server handing out leases and whether the DHCP pools have enough lease capacity.

If you're running DHCP on Linux, chances are you're using ISC's DHCPd. Unfortunately, ISC's DHCPd is a real pain to properly monitor due to how it exposes performance data. In other words, you might have to put in a little bit of work here.

Lease information is stored in */var/lib/dhcpd.leases* (that path might be different depending on your distribution). This file appends new leases to the end, so it's entirely possible (and common) that the file will have two (or more!) leases for the same device, though only one of them is valid (the most recent one). Parsing this will give you the information you're looking for on current lease usage. In order to get the data on the size of the lease pool, you'll need to parse the pool definitions in the main DHCPd config file (*/etc/dhcp/dhcpd.conf*) to get the size of the IP range.

SMTP

If you are running your own email services, then monitoring email is quite important. Email services are generally stable but can quickly ruin your day when things go wrong.

There are a lot of common email server packages out there, so I'll cover the general metrics common to them all.

The outbound email queue measures how much email is waiting to be sent out for delivery. It's best to measure this in relation to what's normal and alert on it when things are abnormal.

Measuring the total amount of email sent and received (both in total and per mailbox) is great for spotting patterns and abnormal behavior (such as a potentially compromised mailbox).

Likewise, the size of mailboxes is a great indicator of how much capacity you need to plan for. I like to measure this both as a total and per-mailbox to spot power users and perhaps help them cut down storage.

Monitoring Scheduled Jobs

One of the trickiest things in monitoring seems like it should be so simple: how to monitor scheduled tasks/cron jobs where an absence of data is the symptom of something awry.

We've all been there before: the backup didn't run and no one noticed for a few weeks. Oops. Now to add in some monitoring so that doesn't happen again...

Since most setups send an email or append to a log on success, it's easy to miss when a failure happens. One way to handle alerting on an absence of data is to create data where there was none before:

```
run-backup.sh 2>&1 backup.log || echo "Job failed" > backup.log
```

This will redirect the script's stderr to stdout and then write both to *backup.log*. This requires that your script implements solid error handling. The second part is the real magic—if: if *run-backup.sh* fails entirely, then `Job failed` is written to *backup.log*.

Once you have this data in your log, you can send it to your log management systems and set up alerts on the data.

In some cases, this approach doesn't work: for whatever reason, you can't turn an absence of data into a presence of data. What you really need is something that can detect when data *doesn't* appear. This situation's solution is commonly known as a *dead man's switch* (*http://bit.ly/2gCYORS*): the default is to do an action, unless something tells it otherwise.

Implementing this in shell is simple enough (*http://bit.ly/2gD3E1H*):

```
#!/bin/sh

# Time in minutes
TIME_LIMIT=$((60*60))

# State file for updating last touch
STATE_FILE=deadman.dat

# Last access time of the state file (in epoch)
last_touch=$(stat -c %Y $STATE_FILE)

# Current time (in epoch)
current_time=$(date +%s)

# How much time is remaining before the switch fires
timeleft=$((current_time - last_touch))

if [ $timeleft -gt $TIME_LIMIT ]; then
  echo "Dead man's switch activated: job failed!"
fi
```

Using this is equally simple: put the code into its own cron job running every minute, then modify the preceding job above like this:

```
run-backup.sh && touch deadman.dat
```

The dead man's switch will now fire automatically if the state file is older than a certain age.

I should caution you this is a naive implementation and could use much improving, but the core idea is sound.

As a bonus, there are hosted services that do this without the need for you to engineer it all yourself. Search Google for cron job monitoring and you'll find many options.

Logging

Logging can be thought of as three separate problems: collection of logs, storage of logs, and analysis of logs.

Collection

I like to group location of logs into two groups: those in syslog and those that aren't.

If your logs are being handled by a syslog daemon already, simply configure the daemon to do log forwarding to another server. Consult your syslog daemon's documentation for specifics on how to do it.

Syslog Forwarding: UDP Versus TCP

There's an ongoing debate about using UDP or TCP for forwarding syslog. On the UDP side, since there's no acknowledgment required, you could send out "the last dying breath" of a server right before it crashes hard. On the TCP side, you get encryption (TLS requires TCP) and assurance that you're not missing any log entries.

I recommend using TCP for two reasons:

1. For most environments, that "last dying breath" isn't useful. Solve for problems you actually have, not for problems you might have in the future.
2. I don't want to lose messages, and syslog encryption is a no-brainer when using SaaS log management.

If your logs aren't being handled by syslog, you have two choices:

1. Update the configuration on whatever it is that's emitting the logs, and have it send them to syslog.
2. Update your syslog configuration to ingest the flat file from disk into syslog. At this point, the log entries are effectively being managed by your syslog daemon and will be forwarded like your other syslog entries.

If you're using a tool that supports the collection of non-syslog log files, then you can use whatever that tool recommends as a third option. There's nothing wrong with that approach at all, though there is something to be said for consistency in how you ingest and send logs.

Storage

Once you're collecting logs, you've got to send them somewhere. In the old days, we would forward all these logs to a central log server that was just a simple syslog receiver and then use standard *NIX tools (e.g., *grep*) to search through logs. This is a suboptimal solution for (at least) one reason: it's hard to search the logs. More often than not, if you're using this method for log storage, no one is looking at them or making use of the logs in any way.

Thankfully, we have lots of great tools available to us now for the storage and analysis of logs. We can split these tools into two categories: SaaS and on-premise.

As you know, I'm a proponent of SaaS monitoring tools. There are also many well-known and capable on-premise tools. I'm not going to make any specific recommendations (you can, however, find many great options with a quick search online). The important part is this: don't send your logs to some syslog server, never to be seen again. Send them to a solid log management system where you can actually get value from them.

Analysis

You're collecting all the logs you want and sending them to a log management service somewhere. Great! Now what?

Now that you've got the plumbing, it's time to do something useful: log analysis.

Analyzing logs isn't a single problem, unfortunately. On one end of the spectrum, you've got shell scripts that grep for certain strings; and on the other end, you have tools like Splunk doing heavy statistical analysis on contents, and everything in between.

There are a great many interesting things you'll find in your logs, most of which will depend entirely on your infrastructure. To get you started, I recommend logging and paying attention to these:

- HTTP responses
- sudo usage
- SSH logins
- cron job results
- MySQL/PostgreSQL slow queries

Analyzing logs is largely a matter of which tool you use, whether it's Splunk, the ELK stack, or some SaaS tool. I strongly encourage you to use a log aggregation tool for analyzing and working with your log data.

Wrap-Up

Whew, what a chapter, eh? We hit a whole lot of topics:

- Why the standard OS metrics aren't as usual for alerts as you might think and how to use them more effectively
- How to monitor the typical services you'll be using: web servers, database servers, load balancers, and others
- What logging looks like from the server perspective

A server is only as reliable as the network on which it depends, so let's dive into the world of weird SNMP and network monitoring.

## CHAPTER 9

Network Monitoring

Network monitoring has a special place in my heart. Starting with my first job in tech, I've been fascinated with how networks worked. I quickly discovered the importance of monitoring: one day while removing some old gear from a closet, I accidentally knocked out the power plug to a switch that was perched precariously on a desk. Given that everyone else had gone home already, this went unnoticed until the next morning, when dozens of people were unable to check their email. I quickly fixed the issue and then searched online for something like "monitor network switch" and then set up Nagios. I've been hooked ever since.

Over my next several jobs as a systems administrator, I gravitated back to network engineering and network monitoring. One thing I've learned over the years is that the behavior and performance of the network is fundamental to the behavior and performance of everything that relies on it—which, these days, is everything. If your network is only capable of maintaining three nines of availability (99.9%), then your applications can't possibly maintain four nines (99.99%). Increasing the availability of the network is a nice lever you pull to allow everything that relies on it to improve.

Networking is one of the few "dark arts" left in the tech world. So many people don't understand it, yet it's a crucial component of everything we do. To the network engineers reading this chapter, this will likely be a recap of things you already know (and hopefully have implemented!). As is often the case with networking though, system administrators, DevOps engineers, and software engineers tend to find themselves doing light network engineering with only a basic understanding of networking. It is my aim to teach the non-network engineers how to properly monitor the network while offering a refresher course for the network engineers among you.

The Pains of SNMP

If you come from a systems or software background, network monitoring can feel like you've stepped back into the stone ages. The biggest challenge in monitoring network performance is due to one simple fact: you have to use SNMP.[1]

Simple Network Management Protocol (SNMP) is a protocol that was simple and revolutionary when it was released but feels esoteric and arcane today. Unfortunately, it's what we've got, so let's dive in.

What Is SNMP?

SNMP (*https://tools.ietf.org/html/rfc1067*) is a protocol proposed under RFC 1067 in 1988 for the purpose of monitoring and managing devices. SNMP was designed for monitoring and management of a wide range of things, and it was common for SNMP to be used on servers as well as network devices. In some older enterprise environments, SNMP on servers is still a common thing (we discussed why this is a bad idea in Chapter 8).

While the world of system administration and software engineering has continually adopted new methods of monitoring and management, network device vendors never really have. There have been a few fits and starts, and some vendors are even supporting popular tools from the server monitoring world such as =collectd=, but by and large, you're stuck with SNMP when it comes to network devices. This is slowly changing, but it's still going to be a while before something other than SNMP is ubiquitous.

How Does It Work?

SNMP is a UDP-based protocol using ports 161 and 162. *Polling* occurs on port 161 (inbound to the device), while *traps* use port 162 (outbound from the device)—we'll cover these two terms shortly. There are many RFCs that define the behavior of SNMP, but they're really not that important for you to know. If you're interested, start at IETF.org and search for SNMP.

There are two key concepts to SNMP communication: the *agent* and the *manager*. The agent is the device you want to get information from, while the manager is the device receiving the information. The agent is a process running on the operating system of the network device you want to query (in SNMP terms, poll), but for our pur-

---

1 To be fair, that's not *completely* true: many network gear vendors are doing a wonderful job at designing devices that look a lot more like servers under the hood, allowing us to make use of standard server monitoring tools instead of SNMP. That said, their market penetration is still low when compared to the majority of companies still using older equipment. SNMP is going to be around a while yet.

poses, you can consider the agent to be a given network device. The manager, being whatever is receiving the information from the agent, is really just any device you're querying SNMP from, whether it's a server in a datacenter or your laptop. Windows, Linux, and OS X all have the capability to be used as an SNMP client (manager) or server (agent).

The agent provides data in a tree format made up of *object IDs* (OIDs). An OID is represented as a series of integers, for example, `.1.3.6.1.2.1.1.1.0`. Note the preceding `.` which represents the root of the object tree. An OID can be translated to a text format, which is significantly easier to understand than a bunch of numbers. After translation, the preceding OID is translated as `sysDescr.0`.

This translation occurs through the use of *Management Information Base* files, commonly known as MIBs. MIBs are stored as flat files on the disk of the SNMP manager and contain a mapping of numerical OIDs to textual representations of the data. These are formatted in a format known as *SMI*, which is a subset of the *ASN.1* format. These formats are complex and take a while to understand, but 99% of you won't need to worry about it. When an SNMP query is made, the manager tools will attempt to translate the OID transparently. As a result, you can query SNMP using the numeric or textual representation, and the returned data will be represented as translated OIDs if the translation was successful.

 Let me distinguish between OIDs and MIBs to clear up a common misunderstanding: an OID is the location in the tree of specific information, while a MIB translates the numeric OID into a textual representation. A MIB is not required to retrieve information from an agent or a given OID.

Though SNMP is most often queried for data, it also supports *traps*. SNMP traps are best thought of as log events. A trap is emitted from the device when an event occurs and is sent to whereever you have configured traps to go. It's been my experience that any data in an SNMP trap can also be found in the device's syslog, so I tend to disable traps entirely. If you want to use them, I recommend sending them to a log server that is set up to accept them. If you're using a commercial piece of software for handling SNMP traps, follow that software's instructions. If you want to use something open source, I recommend *snmptrapd* from the *net-snmp* package; you can find configuration instructions for it in *net-snmp*'s documentation.

There is no standard implementation for an SNMP agent. Each vendor implements it the way they want, though most try to conform to the RFCs with varying levels of success. There is no list of objects an SNMP agent is required to implement, though most vendors will implement sysDescr.0 (the description of the device, usually make and model) at minimum.

There are multiple versions of SNMP in use, with each one providing slightly different capabilities:

Version 1

Version 1 was introduced in 1988. Security was accomplished through the use of a *community string*, which is essentially a password. Community strings are passed in plain text over the network. One particularly notable aspect of v1 is that counter objects were only 32-bit, which means that counters with lots of changes (e.g., "high speed" network links) would "wrap" quickly—that is, they would simply hit their max and reset to zero. For most network links found today, the counter may wrap multiple times in mere minutes, possibly between polling intervals, resulting in a severe distortion of the rate of change.

Version 2

Version 2, introduced in 1993, solved some of the problems with version 1, most notably adding support for 64-bit counters to solve the 32-bit counter wrap issue. Version 2 also introduced "bulk requests," which allowed for requesting large sets of OIDs at once as well as a new user-based security model. Ultimately, the user-based security model turned out to be unpopular, and version 2c was quickly introduced. version 2 is uncommon, and most vendors implement version 2c and call it Version 2.

Version 2c

Version 2c, introduced in 1996, went back to the community string security model. This version, known colloquially as "v2c" is the most common and widely adopted.

Version 3

Version 3, introduced in 2002, is the latest version of the SNMP protocol. It re-introduced an updated version of the user-based security model as well as encryption and a few other enhancements. Some smaller vendors still do not support v3, despite being introduced over a decade ago, though most major network vendors offer full support for it.

A Word on Security

SNMP is an inherently insecure protocol. Community strings are passed in plain text, as well as requests and responses, which may include sensitive data (such as hostnames and phone numbers). SNMP v3 attempts to solve some of these problems by encrypting requests/responses and using a user-based security model, but v3 places more load on network devices and sometimes isn't supported.

Generally speaking, the best way to secure SNMP is to architect security into your infrastructure, knowing that you're going to have an insecure protocol in use on it. The best way to do this is to build a management network into your architecture and allow SNMP queries to happen on the interfaces on that network only. It is not advised to allow SNMP on unprotected networks.

 Most network device operating systems de-prioritize the SNMP agent when the device is under heavy load, which will cause your SNMP querics to be slow. Unfortunately, a device under heavy load is precisely when you want more visibility, not less. C'est la vie.

How Do I Use SNMP?

Many network monitoring packages contain functionality for using SNMP and often have many prebuilt queries and dashboards for common objects such as network interfaces, so I'm not going to cover those. Instead, I'm going to cover using SNMP from the command line, which is useful for fleshing out new queries and trouble-shooting SNMP. Note that this is for Linux and OS X—sorry Windows users, you're on your own.

Installation and configuration on Linux

Install the `net-snmp` package using the package manager for your distro. For Debian/Ubuntu:

```
apt-get install snmp
```

and for RedHat/CentOS:

```
yum install net-snmp net-snmp-utils
```

Once you have `net-snmp` installed, you're going to want MIBs. On Debian/Ubuntu, a collection of MIBs can be had by installing a separate package:

```
apt-get install snmp-mibs-downloader
```

then running as root:

```
download-mibs
```

Finally, edit */etc/snmp/snmp.conf* and ensure `mibs +ALL` is in the file. For RedHat/CentOS, MIBs are included in the packages.

Installation configuration on macOS

Using homebrew, install the `net-snmp` package:

```
brew install net-snmp
```

This package will automatically set up the tools and the MIBs, so no additional configuration is required.

Testing

You can test that the SNMP agent is working from your manager by running:

```
snmpstatus -c <community string> -v 2c <hostname>
```

You can test translation by running:

```
snmpget -c <community string> -v 2c <hostname> sysDescr.0
```

It should return something like this:

```
SNMPv2-MIB::sysDescr.0 = STRING: <text here>
```

If it isn't working, it will return an error:

```
sysDescr.0: Unknown Object Identifier (Sub-id not found: (top) -> sysDescr)
```

In the case of the error, ensure your configuration of *∕etc∕snmp∕snmp.conf* is correct and you've installed the MIB package.

net-snmp

The net-snmp tools contain several command line utilities of varying usefulness. The most useful are *snmpget* and *snmpwalk*.

snmpget retrieves a single OID, while snmpwalk will enumerate an entire tree of OIDs. For example, let's consider a device with multiple network interfaces:

```
~$ snmpwalk -c <community string> -v 2c <hostname> IF-MIB::ifDescr
IF-MIB::ifDescr.1 = STRING: lo
IF-MIB::ifDescr.2 = STRING: Red Hat, Inc Device 0001
IF-MIB::ifDescr.3 = STRING: Red Hat, Inc Device 0001
```

In this example, I've "walked" the ifDescr table and now have a list of each of the network interfaces the SNMP agent knows about. The numbers at the end of the OID are called indexes and are an important concept for SNMP. For single-item OIDs, such as sysDescr, the index number is 0. The actual OID for sysDescr is .1.3.6.1.2.1.1.1.0, which translates to sysDescr.0. When there is only a single item in a tree, the SNMP manager tools will automatically return that item. However, if you try to retrieve an OID that contains multiple items underneath, the behavior is different and a little misleading:

```
~$ snmpget -c <community string> -v 2c <hostname> IF-MIB::ifDescr
IF-MIB::ifDescr = No Such Instance currently exists at this OID
```

This is different from the behavior we saw when we walked that OID, and that's due to this OID being a *table*, that is, a collection of items. It can be hard to predict whether an OID is a table or a single item, so just make your best guess. Generally, if you expect there to be multiple items underneath, it's probably a table.

Let's see what happens when we retrieve ifDescr for the second index:

```
~$ snmpget -c <community string> -v 2c <hostname> IF-MIB::ifDescr.2
IF-MIB::ifDescr.2 = STRING: Red Hat, Inc Device 0001
```

Perfecto. We've now retrieved a single item from the network interfaces table.

There are other useful commands in net-snmp as well. snmpstatus is great for testing whether SNMP is functioning, as it queries several OIDs; and *snmptranslate* will translate a given numeric OID to the textual representation without querying a device. You can read all about the available options and commands by running man snmpcmd.

Installing vendor MIBs

You will undoubtedly need to add MIBs you get from your vendor to your manager machine. Doing so is straightforward: create a directory somewhere (it doesn't matter where) and then add a new line to *etc/snmp/snmp.conf* before mibs +ALL: **mibdirs <path to your MIB folder>**. Place all your vendor MIBs in this folder, and SNMP will automatically pick them up.

The net-snmp client does not recursively search directories for MIBs, so if you're like me and want to organize your MIB collection by vendor, simply create one folder per vendor under your new MIB directory and then add those folders individually to your mibdirs configuration entry like so:

```
mibdirs /opt/vendor-mibs/cisco /opt/vendor-mibs/juniper /opt/vendor-mibs/avaya
```

That's great, Mike. But where's the list of OIDs I should monitor?

I'm glad you asked!

There isn't one. Nor could I possibly give you a master list without it being out of date by the time this book goes to print.

By teaching you how SNMP works and how to use the net-snmp command line tools, I've given you the capability to search through an agent's supported OIDs yourself. When you come upon a new device (or even an updated firmware of an old device), you'll have the knowledge you need to go through the OIDs and find the data you want.

Now that we've gotten SNMP out of the way, let's get down to business: what should you be monitoring and why?

Interface Metrics

We'll start with the obvious one: interfaces.

Network performance comes down to a few key factors: *bandwidth*, *throughput*, *latency*, *errors*, and *jitter*.

Bandwidth

>The theoretical maximum amount of information that can be pushed through a connection at once. Think of this as raw capability of a network link. This is commonly expressed in bits per second, usually megabits per second (Mbps) or gigabits per second (Gbps). This is not to be confused with megabytes per second (MBps) or gigabytes per second (GBps).

Throughput

>The observed performance of a network link, also expressed in bits per second. Due to protocol and transmission overhead, throughput will be less than the link's bandwidth. For example, assuming a standard Ethernet link with a 1,500 byte MTU, the max throughput of a TCP stream is limited to about 95% of the bandwidth due to overhead from Ethernet, IP, and TCP encapsulations. The more encapsulation you're doing (e.g., MPLS) the less efficiency you'll have. If you're only getting 60% during tests, then you've probably got an issue somewhere.

>Monitoring the throughput of a link is important to ensuring you're getting the most out of it. Simply recording the octets via the IF-MIB MIB and comparing against the known max of that link won't be sufficient, as that's only going to measure throughput at that moment in time.

>Instead, you need to perform a test. You can use a tool like *iperf2* (*https://github.com/esnet/iperf*) to do such a test or opt for the *bwctl* package from the folks at Internet2 (*https://software.internet2.edu/bwctl/*), which is designed as a suite of tools for testing network performance. Bonus points for being able to automate the test and store the results over time. Strategically placing test endpoints around your network will enable you to consistently keep an eye on critical network link performance.

>If you suspect you should be getting more throughput out of it than you are, you can check for some errors: drops and overruns can indicate a saturated network link, while collisions can indicate duplex mismatches (on a full duplex connection). Of course, physical issues can also impact performance, so be sure you're monitoring for those.

Confusingly, server administrators often talk about bandwidth and throughput in bytes per second (Bps), while network engineers talk about it in bits per second (bps). Be aware of this communication hurdle when interacting between teams. You can easily convert bps to Bps by dividing the number by eight, or by Bps to bps by multiplying by eight.

Measuring Throughput

There are two main ways to measure throughput: SNMP counters or a tool like `iperf2`. If you're using SNMP counters, they automatically take into account any overhead, while tools like `iperf2` do not. There's nothing inherently bad about either one, but be aware that you'll see different numbers with `iperf2` than from your SNMP counters.

Latency

The time it takes a packet to travel across a network link. Lower is better, of course, but there's still a physical limitation on latency due to how fast electricity (or light, in the case of fiber optic cables) can travel.

Latency can have a big impact on the user experience in some applications that are not tolerant of high latency. One of my favorite ways to monitor latency between two points is to use tools such as `iperf2` or *smokeping* (*http:// oss.oetiker.ch/smokeping/*) to regularly measure and report latency. After carefully placing a few of these servers in your infrastructure, you'll be able to graph and alert on latency.

Errors

Include metrics such as Rx/Tx errors, drops, CRC errors, overruns, carrier errors, resets, and collisions. Consult your network device for how each of these are exposed—some vendors don't provide them at all.

Usually, Rx/Tx errors are exposed by default in the IF-MIB SNMP table, but depending on the agent implementation, it may include the other error metrics, or it may not. Typically, Rx/Tx errors are an aggregate of error metrics and aren't reliable for determining what is wrong, just that something is. The more specific error counters are far more useful for diagnostics and alerting. I tend to ignore Rx/Tx errors in favor of the other error metrics, if they're available.

The most common thing you'll want to monitor for are physical issues: electrical interference and bad transceivers/cables can degrade network performance quickly. You can monitor for this via CRC errors and carrier errors. If you have fiber in your network, light levels are also very important.

Jitter

The deviation of a metric from its usual measurement. In networking, jitter is most commonly applied to latency measurements. For example, latency swings from 1 ms to 150 ms to 30 ms would be an example of high jitter, while a constant 3 ms latency would be no jitter at all. Jitter is important in interactive voice and audio infrastructures, as it will cause the stream to come across as sounding and looking broken or choppy. You can pay attention to latency jitter by monitoring latency and checking for inconsistency.

I'm a big fan of metaphors and explaining these concepts in a metaphor is one of my favorite ways to teach it. A good way of thinking about these metrics goes like this:

Imagine a highway with four lanes across—that's the bandwidth. Increasing the number of lanes increases bandwidth, but it does not necessarily increase throughput, which is the number of vehicles that travel down the highway in a given time period.

Latency is the length of the highway. No matter how many lanes you give the highway, you still aren't changing how long it takes to travel down it.

Errors can be anything from a car crash to someone stopping unexpectedly in traffic, causing a traffic jam. Jitter is how regular the time it takes to get down the highway is —if it's unpredictable, that's high jitter.

If the highway is constantly full, it's taking much longer to get from point A to point B. If there are errors (slowdowns, crashes), you might be able to solve this by adding another lane, but there are clearly limitations to that: you can only build a highway so big, not to mention the cost of doing so. Sometimes there are no errors at all and traffic is flowing smoothly—in this case, you've got perfect utilization.

Interface and Logging

The syslog for a device also contains information about what interfaces are doing (though you can also get this information from your configuration tracking tool, if you're using one). You're specifically going to be interested in these events:

- Changes to trunk ports
- Ports becoming err-disabled
- Link aggregated interfaces becoming bundled or unbundled

Recap

Here's my rule of thumb: monitor and alert on the interfaces used for uplinks and servers. It's up to you as to whether you feel it's necessary to monitor access ports at all (desktops, laptops), but I normally don't bother: access ports are noisy and flap

---

often, giving you not a lot of useful information. Don't forget about your aggregated ports either—they're good to keep track of.

Configuration Tracking

Tracking configuration changes to your network devices is one of the highest-impact things you can be doing. How many times has an incident happened in your network, and you found out that it was the result of a change that someone made last week but no one knew about it?

Tools such as RANCID (*http://www.shrubbery.net/rancid/*) function by logging into your devices with a read-only account, downloading the config, and putting it into a version control system. Thanks to version control, the configuration is stored over time as it changes. Every time the config changes, you and your team can be notified via email, Slack, or any other method you choose. With tools like these, you'll never again wonder what change was made and how to roll it back. Every single one of you should be tracking configuration changes to your devices.

Voice and Video

Monitoring voice and video performance can be tricky. Due to the codecs being encrypted, it's rather difficult to observe connection quality from the outside. Thankfully, most vendors provide some sort of monitoring tools with their products for in-depth analysis. Given that, we'll cover only the general approach common to all video and voice monitoring.

As you know, I'm a big fan of starting your monitoring from the user's perspective. When it comes to the performance of voice and video streams, however, there's not a lot you can do thanks to how they work. On the upside, there's also not a lot that can go wrong with them.

Voice and video performance is all about three measurements: latency, jitter, and packet loss. Video and voice are quite sensitive to these metrics and will perform best with the lowest numbers possible. We've already covered how to monitor these metrics in this chapter.

Another particularly important thing to monitor is the codec in use: it should be the same across the network. If it's not, this can cause performance issues. You can check the codec in use via SNMP. In theory, the codec won't change once it's set, but we all know permanent things have a tendency to change when we least expect it.

Due to the performance-sensitive nature of voice and video, the internal networks will often have *Quality-of-Service* (QoS) policies applied in order to ensure they receive priority treatment and preserve the quality of the streams, which most vendors will expose via SNMP. In the Cisco world, QoS metrics are described by the

Cisco Class-Based QoS Configuration and Statistics MIB (*http://bit.ly/2zExk5T*). This is a rather complex SNMP object, and trying to sift through it by hand is an effort in futility and madness if you have a lot of policies defined. If you're attempting to monitor QoS at any sort of scale, I recommend having a chat with your network gear vendor and asking them what tools they recommend (Googling for `QoS monitoring` will also suffice).

One particularly interesting capability is Cisco's IP SLA. IP SLA, once configured, will simulate traffic and report back with results on how it performed. IP SLA results can trigger alerts, be monitored via SNMP, and even cause actions to occur, such as informing routing protocols that a path should change to avoid problem segments.

Routing

Monitoring your routing protocols can be an interesting challenge. Dynamic routing protocols, by design, are meant to be self-healing, making the determination of when to alert someone rather tricky. For multi-homed networks, is it worth waking someone up over a BGP peer change? Probably not. What about for dual-homed networks? Probably so. The same is true for monitoring OSPF neighbor changes: it all depends.

Most of the useful monitoring to be had here is for the dynamic routing protocols (OSPF and BGP, primarily). Monitoring static routes is better achieved by monitoring the underlying links and the ability to pass traffic over the route (e.g., using `iperf2`) than by monitoring for the existence of the route.

When it comes to BGP, there's a lot you can and should monitor:

- Size of the TCAM table in relation to the size of the chassis's memory. Maxing this out can be lead to a very bad day, as evidenced by the TCAM exhaustion for some Cisco devices back in 2014 that led to outages at many large companies (*http://bit.ly/2gAY6Vj*).
- BGP peer changes
- BGP AS path change (this can be useful for some especially latency-sensitive organizations)
- BGP community changes (number of prefixes being sent and received by peers)

OSPF has comparatively few things to worry about: adjacency changes are about it, which you can find in both syslog and SNMP.

Finally, monitoring changes in first-hop redundancy can be a good indicator of behavior change in your network. SNMP exposes VRRP and HSRP members, as well as which of them is the active member. The router's syslog will also report when the active member changes.

Spanning Tree Protocol (STP)

Spanning tree changes can wreak havoc on a network in a hurry. On Cisco devices, spanning tree logs can be enabled at the device level, which contain useful information about protocol and spanning tree roots, but this is only available at the debug log level (which can cause excessive load on a busy switch). Enabling it at the interface level provides less information, but contains most of what we want to keep track of: that a change happened.

When it comes to spanning tree, we want to know only two things: when a root bridge changes and when the protocol reconverges. Root bridge changes are something that should happen rarely, if ever, in a relatively static network, so you'll want to know that they've occurred via an alert (though perhaps not a wake-me-up alert). Protocol changes are somewhat more normal and acceptable, so what you'll want to look for there is patterns and how often they occur. One great way to do that is to have your log management service count the number of protocol change events and graph them in your metrics service.

Chassis

I've found that people spend so much time working out how to monitor interfaces that they forget entirely about the chassis of the devices.

CPU and Memory

Graphing CPU and memory usage can be good indicators of load, but they can just as often be red herrings. I once had a set of chassis switches that alternated between 1% and 100% CPU utilization every few minutes, which was considered normal for the switch. On the other, another chassis switch tended to run at 100% CPU utilization, which the vendor also called normal. So, graph them, but take the data with a grain of salt, and certainly don't alert on them (unless your vendor advises it).

Some line cards and supervisor cards also include their own on-card memory and CPU. It's entirely possible for CPU or memory on a card to be exhausted while the chassis appears idle. Make sure you're monitoring *all* CPU and memory instances.

Hardware

Don't forget about the actual hardware of your devices. Monitoring switch stacks, line cards, supervisor cards, and power supplies is crucial, though many devices don't expose all of this information.

One important thing to look for is cold start messages in your syslog. Cold starts represent a device having rebooted and is absolutely something you should be paying attention to.

Flow Monitoring

Most network device vendors support flow monitoring with sFlow (open standard), IPFIX (open standard), NetFlow (*http://bit.ly/2yPdzeJ*) (Cisco), or jFlow (Juniper).

A flow, as defined by Cisco, is a unidirectional sequence of packets that all share seven common values:

1. Ingress interface (SNMP ifIndex)
2. Source IP address
3. Destination IP address
4. IP protocol
5. Source port for UDP or TCP, 0 for other protocols
6. Destination port for UDP or TCP, type and code for ICMP, or 0 for other protocols
7. IP type of service

Flow monitoring is great for tracking down such things as high-bandwidth activities or nodes or analyzing bandwidth utilization on a per-IP, per-protocol, per-application, or per-service basis.

There are a few different implementations with different behavior between them:

NetFlow
> A proprietary Cisco standard, available in v5 and v9 variants. Not all Cisco devices support NetFlow.

sFlow
> sFlow stands for *sampled flow* and differs from NetFlow in that it's designed to *sample* flows, rather than collect every last one like NetFlow (though NetFlow *can* be configured for sampling). Essentially, sFlow *has* to sample flows, while NetFlow *can* sample flows. This sampling improves performance of flow collection at the expense of accuracy.

J-Flow
> Juniper's brand of a flow monitoring solution in v5, v8, and v9 variants. Functionally identical to sFlow.

IPFIX
> An open standard for flow monitoring based on NetFlow v9.

One of the useful things about sFlow that I like is that it also contains octet information for every interface. As sFlow is push-based, you can have this information pushed to a receiver for recording in a metrics system elsewhere. As an example of this, Jason Dixon wrote an sFlow receiver (*https://github.com/obfuscurity/evenflow*) in Ruby that exports to Graphite; this could be easily adapted to your needs.

If you want to do flow analysis on a busy network, I recommend looking for devices that will collect flows in a hardware solution, to keep the load down on your routers.

 The information flows contain can often be sensitive. It is not advised to use flow monitoring on publicly accessible networks.

Capacity Planning

Before we wrap up this chapter, let's talk a bit about capacity planning and how network monitoring helps this task. Capacity planning can be performed two primary ways:

- Starting with a business requirement and working backward
- Forecasting based on usage

Working Backward

This method is often used for when the business has hard requirements, and you need to determine how to implement. For example, if the business requires that a certain amount of data be transferred elsewhere within a certain amount of time, you can work backward to determine what size links are required to accomplish the goal. This method is not informed by any monitoring data.

Forecasting

Forecasting, on the other hand, requires the use of data you've been storing in your monitoring system. This method is often used on a regular basis to upgrade links and hardware as the utilization grows over time. Some organizations opt to simply purchase the best hardware or links they can for the money they have budgeted, while others prefer to make decisions based on current and forecasted usage.

If you're making data-based decisions, your forecasting is straightforward: take at least the last six months of data and apply a trend line for the next however-many months. You have a few options for applying the trend line:

- Export the data to Excel, and use Excel's built-in graphing functionality.
- If you're using rrdtool (*http://bit.ly/2z5Eyn9*), it has built-in trend line/forecasting functionality.

- If you're using Graphite (*http://bit.ly/2gBxtj7*), it also has built-in trend line/fore-casting functionality.

Wrap-up

Monitoring the network is far more complex and involved than many realize, especially at large scale. Let's recap what we've learned in this chapter:

- SNMP is an archaic pain in the rear, but it's what we've got. Make sure to call your vendors and register your displeasure over the lack of a better monitoring and management interface.
- Tracking configuration changes yields lots of great information and can save you time and headaches.
- We learned the intricacies of monitoring interfaces, routing protocols, switching, and chassis components.
- We learned about monitoring the performance of voice and video streams, quality-of-service, and IP SLA.
- Monitoring entire flows using NetFlow, J-Flow, sFlow, and IPFIX gives you deeper understanding of what's happening on your network.
- We learned the fundamentals of capacity planning for network engineering.

We've reached the end of the technical stack, so the next chapter is going to bring us back up to a bird's-eye view where we'll discuss security monitoring for the entire stack.

## CHAPTER 10

Security Monitoring

Security monitoring is a different beast than you're familiar with if you're coming from an infrastructure or application background. When it comes to monitoring an infrastructure, you're instrumenting things that already exist. For example, your web servers already emit health and metrics data, and it's a simple matter to store them and set up any necessary alerts. However, when it comes to security, many people find that the infrastructure and application weren't built with security in mind. There are no existing hooks to use, leaving many engineers in the unfortunate position of having to bolt on security after the fact—not fun.

In some cases, there are entire classes of problems that no one solved for. As an example, how are you going to detect different DDoS signatures if you have no DDoS protection in place to begin with? As a result, unlike previous chapters, this chapter will straddle the line between how to build basic security and how to monitor it. There will be plenty of security approaches and tools I either gloss over or fail to mention—security monitoring is a specialized field unto itself and one that I cannot possibly do justice to in such a short chapter. If you find yourself interested in security monitoring and want to go deeper, I have found Richard Bejtlich's *The Practice of Network Security Monitoring* (No Starch Press, 2013) to be invaluable.

Security is a matter of assessing threat and risk and deciding on compromises. Think of security as a continuum: on one end you have "wet paper bag," and on the other you have "Fort Knox." You wouldn't implement Fort Knox–level security for storing $100, nor would you leave it in the open on the center console of your car while shopping at the mall. In these cases, you're assessing the threat (theft of your $100) and the level of risk (leaving it unattended while shopping at the mall). It doesn't make sense to spend $1,000 to protect against losing $100.

In other cases, the level of security is too intrusive and cumbersome on how you work. Can you imagine if you had the same level of security at home as found at the

White House? Wearing a badge around the house at all times, checking in and out with security staff, pat-downs, metal detectors, bulletproof glass…seems a bit much for the home, right? A good lock on the doors and windows would work much better for the annoyance factor. Many of you work in offices with a higher level of security than you have home: you've got the badge readers at external doors and often even security staff to check in with. The level of annoyance you're comfortable dealing with is higher there, too.

Not all the ideas and tips here will suit everyone—some of it may be too intrusive on workflows or too costly to implement and manage—and that's totally fine. It's important that you consciously make this decision instead of absently deciding that security is too difficult.

With that, let's get started.

Monitoring and Compliance

There are several compliance regulations out there for different industries and different types of companies. You may have heard of a few and might even be involved with ensuring your company's compliance. Some of the most common ones are HIPAA (protection of health care data), Sarbanes-Oxley aka SOX (protection of financials in public companies), PCI-DSS (protection of credit card data), and SOC2 (protection of non-financial controls). While my initial inclination was to list specific things that you should monitor when it comes to compliance, I quickly realized that the answer is "basically everything," making that idea a non-starter.

Well, not quite. To be more specific, anything that falls in scope of a particular regulation should also have a monitoring component built into it. This is to meet the common requirement of compliance that you also demonstrate the control is working the way you think it is working—what better way to prove that than with monitoring?

Some common requirements:

```
1.3.5 Permit only "established" connections into the network.
```

```
(PCI-DSS v3.2)
```

You could prove this control is functioning by monitoring all connections by type at the edge firewall:

```
5.2 Ensure that all anti-virus mechanisms are maintained as follows:
```

- Are kept current,

- Perform periodic scans

- Generate audit logs which are retained per PCI DSS Requirement 10.7.

Prove this control by storing the audit logs in your log aggregation system and monitoring that all nodes are both updating regularly and scans are both starting and finishing:

> (b) Standard: Audit controls. Implement hardware, software, and/or procedural mechanisms that record and examine activity in information systems that contain or use electronic protected health information.
>
> HIPAA, 2007

Simple enough: log everything. (Wait a minute—didn't we learn that logging *everything* is kinda hard? OK, maybe this isn't so simple.)

Achieving compliance often ranges from straightforward to nightmarish, but remember that for most controls, implementing monitoring is a great way to ensure things are working as you hope they are.

User, Command, and Filesystem Auditing

auditd is a userspace interface to the *Linux Audit System*, a component direct hooks to the Linux kernel, allowing it to report on events and actions that occur on the system. The Linux Audit System is built for security uses and is separate from other systems, allowing it to keep functioning even when other subsystems aren't working (such as syslog).

auditd is great for tracking user actions and other events through its high level of configurability. For example, some of the types of events it can report on:

- All sudo executions, the command executed, and who did it
- File access or changes to specific files, when, and by whom
- User authentication attempts and failures

Setting Up auditd

Modern CentOS and Debian-based distributions often have auditd already running. You can have a look at what auditd is logging in */var/log/audit/audit.log*. By default, auditd doesn't log a whole lot (sudo, authentication attempts, a few other things). You can add your own custom rules in */etc/audit/rules.d/audit.rules* (RedHat) or */etc/audit/audit.rules* (Debian). As an example, here's a rule that will monitor all write access to */etc/myconfig.conf*: *-w /etc/myconfig.conf -p wa -k myconfig_changes*.

-w says to watch a file, -p tells auditd which attributes to watch (write and append), and -k is an arbitrary identifier.

Looking in the audit log after making a small change to the config, here's what we see:

```
type=CONFIG_CHANGE msg=audit(1485289062.091:184): auid=1001 ses=844
op="updated_rules" path="/etc/myconfig.conf" key="myconfig_changes" list=4
res=1

type=SYSCALL msg=audit(1485289062.091:185): arch=c000003e syscall=82
success=yes exit=0 a0=55892a3bc880 a1=55892a3b0170 a2=fffffffffffffeb8
a3=55892a3b0160 items=4 ppid=15788 pid=17066 auid=1001 uid=0 gid=0 euid=0
suid=0 fsuid=0 egid=0 sgid=0 fsgid=0 tty=pts0 ses=844 comm="vim"
exe="/usr/bin/vim.basic" key="myconfig_changes"
```

auditd is rather verbose in its logging but there it is: it logged the file change. With a bit more work put into the configuration and tuning of the auditd rules, you can bring the the verbosity under more control and turn it into something very useful. I encourage you to read up on its usage for yourself. A great resource is RedHat's own documentation. auditd ships with example configurations as well, which you can find at */usr/share/doc/auditd/examples/*.

auditd and Remote Logs

One limitation of auditd is that the logs remain local to the server. Since we want to ensure that logs aren't tampered with, we need to make sure they get sent automatically to a central server for aggregation and analysis. To do that, we'll use an auditd plugin called audisp-remote. This plugin allows us to forward auditd events to a remote syslog receiver.

Why Not Use rsyslog to Ingest the Logs?

One question that comes up occasionally is why use audisp-remote at all when rsyslog (or syslogd/syslog-ng) can ingest the audit logs and forward them along with the rest of the server's logs? One configuration is better than two, after all.

While this would work from a technical perspective, it fails the security perspective: since auditd is not reliant on the syslog subsystem to be functioning, auditd can continue to record and forward audit events to a remote server even if rsyslog is disabled (such as when a malicious user has intentionally disabled it). It's not foolproof (they could disable audisp-remote as well), but it's an extra level of protection.

If you do go the syslog route, you can use the audisp-syslog plugin to send auditd logs to syslog, or you can ingest directly via rsyslog/syslog-ng from file (*/var/log/audit/audit.log*).

Setting up audisp-remote is simple. You will need to install the *audispd-plugins* package. Once that's installed, edit */etc/audisp/audispd-remote.conf* and change the remote_server and port configuration directives to your remote syslog server. Audit logs should now be forwarding to your remote log server. If not, check the main syslog log file (*/var/log/messages* or */var/log/syslog* depending on your distribution) for errors.

Once you have logs aggregated in one place, you start searching and setting up alerts on interesting events. Some common things I recommend to watch for are successful SSH logins and failed and successful sudo attempts. Once you start looking at the logs, you'll no doubt find other interesting things to keep an eye on.

One final note: there are now SaaS tools on the market that will do the collection, aggregation, and analysis of `auditd` logs for you, making this whole exercise as simple as a few lines of configuration. A couple of the well-known examples of this are `Cloud Passage` and `ThreatStack`.

Host Intrusion Detection System (HIDS)

A *host intrusion detection system* (HIDS) detects bad actors on a particular host. There are many HIDSs out there, all with different focuses. In this section, we're going to focus on a simple yet broad one: *rootkits*.

Before we get into detecting rootkits, what in the world are they? I happen to like Wikipedia's definition the best:

> A rootkit is a collection of computer software, typically malicious, designed to enable access to a computer or areas of its software that would not otherwise be allowed (for example, to an unauthorized user) and often masks its existence or the existence of other software.
>
> —McAfee (via Wikipedia)

Rootkits can be anything from mass-installed PHP-based webshells to stealthy recompiled system binaries and everything in-between. Due to their stealthy nature, detecting rootkits can be rather difficult, requiring you to rely on many strategies: user/process behavior analysis, log analysis, file system and process auditing, file hash comparisons, and much more.

rkhunter

`rkhunter` is a popular and proven tool for the detection of rootkits. It does its job through many different strategies such as file hash comparisons from known-good hashes, signature-based detection of known rootkits, and some standard best practice security checks (such as whether root SSH is allowed).

Installing and configuring rkhunter is simple: install the `rkhunter` package. After installation, run *rkhunter --update* to ensure it updates the signature database followed by *rkhunter --propupd* to update the file properties database. Now you're ready for your first run. To kick it off, run: *rkhunter -c.*

This will output all the checks its running to stdout. It will also log both the checks and the results to */var/log/rkhunter.log*. Of course, since we're all big fans of automation, this manual process won't do for production uses.

Thankfully, the folks behind rkhunter have taken care of that for us too with a few flags: `--cronjob` and `--quiet`.

Simply put this into a cron job (I recommend at least once a day): */usr/bin/rkhunter --cronjob --update --quiet.*

You'll notice I've added the `--update` flag. This ensures that rkhunter will always use the latest database of checks every time it runs. You can also add the `--syslog` flag to log the start and end time to syslog.

I recommend sending the log file to your remote log aggregation/analysis system where you can set up some alerts. For any issues rkhunter finds, it will prefix them with `Warning`, so you can set up an alert on that. I would also consider setting up an alert for the absence of rkhunter running, which you can do by searching for `Info: Start date is` and sending an alert if it hasn't shown up within the time frame it should have.

If you're looking for tools that are more robust than `rkhunter`, I recommend looking into OSSEC (*https://ossec.github.io/*).

Network Intrusion Detection System (NIDS)

A *network intrusion detection system* (NIDS) is quite useful for detecting threats on the network itself (as opposed to on a host, which is the purview of a *host intrusion detection system—HIDS*). A NIDS works by listening in on the raw traffic on the wire using one or more *network taps* placed throughout the network.

Whereas a firewall performs proactive intrusion prevention by blocking access attempts according to defined filters (access control lists, typically), a NIDS reports on intrusions after they have occurred. At first glance, you might wonder why that's helpful—after all, shouldn't we focus on preventing intrusions?

That's true: we should put focus on securing our networks to prevent intrusions in the first place—but intrusions are inevitable. This is where a NIDS comes into play. If you do indeed put effort into securing your network at the edges but also assume your network will be breached anyway (spoiler: it will), a NIDS allows you to spot the threats and react quickly.

To make the most of a NIDS deployment, you need *network taps*. A network tap is a piece of hardware that sits inline on your network, intercepting all traffic that passes through it and forwarding a copy to another system.

Placing network taps is a strategic choice. You want them placed at network choke points and demarcation points where it can intercept all traffic from that segment. In simple networks, you might have only a single tap sitting downstream of a router/ firewall. In more complex enterprise networks, you might have hundreds of taps scattered in various places. Figure 10-1 shows an example of network tap placement.

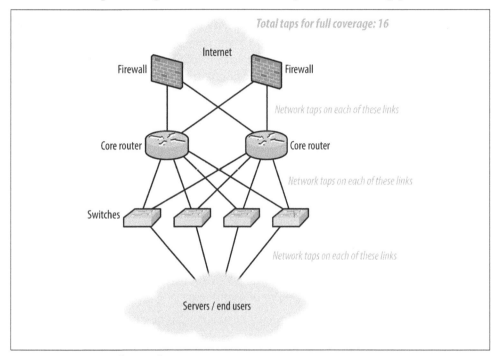

Figure 10-1. Network tap placement

 Because a network tap is placed inline on a network link, make sure you monitor the tap for availability as well as taking care to choose taps that are reliable and have a *fail-open* failure mode (that is, when they die, they act as a coupler between two network cables instead of shutting down the link).

Span Ports or Hardware Taps?

One question that often comes up when discussing network taps is the debate between using span ports/port mirroring versus hardware network taps.

My recommendation is to use hardware taps. Because a span port is a single network port on a switch, it is easy to overwhelm the port with traffic, whereas a network tap is designed to handle much higher levels of traffic.

Once you've got network taps deployed, you need a place to send the traffic for analysis, a tool called a *security information and event management* (SIEM) system. There are several open source and commercial tools available that function as SIEMs, such as Bro and Snort (both open source). While configuring a NIDS is beyond the scope of this chapter, know that like any other monitoring tool, it requires regular tuning to get the most out of it.

Wrap-Up

We've hardly touched the wide domain of security monitoring, but I'm confident what we have worked through will give you a solid start on monitoring the security of your applications and infrastructure. To recap:

- Monitoring requirements for compliance purposes are often more straightforward than they appear, though they may not always be *easy*.

- User, command, and file system auditing with auditd is simple to get running but can be a real bear to tweak to a point of usefulness.

- Detecting rootkits and other host-level intrusions can be difficult, but rkhunter is a great starting point.

- Firewalls aren't enough for network security. Careful placement of network taps and NIDS will yield a wealth of information.

This chapter marks the end of our journey into the specifics of how to monitor the various parts of your environment. As a final recap, we'll conduct our own monitoring assessment on my favorite website of all time, *Tater.ly*.

## CHAPTER 11

Conducting a Monitoring Assessment

We've reached the final chapter of the book, folks. You have, I hope, learned many new things. This last chapter will take you through a fictionalized example of applying all the lessons of this book at once using an exercise I do with my own consulting clients: a monitoring assessment.

Performing a monitoring assessment on your environment is a great way to systematically determine what you should be monitoring and why. The end result is a clearer understanding of the behavior of your app and underlying infrastructure. It's by no means exhaustive or perfect, but rather, it's intended to be a starting point to get you thinking about what matters and what doesn't.

Business KPIs

To start off, we need to figure out exactly what *Tater.ly* does. After a chat with the CEO, we've learned the following:

> *Tater.ly*'s mission is to help french-fry aficionados find the best french fries in all the land. Users come to *Tater.ly* to look up restaurants and read reviews about their french fries, as well as post their own reviews. The french fries are also rated on a scale of one to five, with five being the best. Restaurants can create their own pages or users can create them. Restaurants can "claim" their pages if the page already exists. *Tater.ly* makes money through advertising by placing a *Featured Fry* at the top of search results, with restaurants paying an advertising fee for the slot. The ad fees are based on number of impressions—that is, the number of people that see the ad (as opposed to "clicks," that is, the number of people who click on the ad). Because the ad price is based on impressions, restaurant owners can choose how much to spend and whether to show their ad at peak times or non-peak times. It also allows us to run multiple ads. Currently, *Tater.ly* has gross revenue of $250,000 annually, and that's steadily increasing.

Now that we have have enough information to begin our assessment, let's start with the business metrics: what are the business KPIs?

To start off, there are some basic metrics that tell us the state of the venture:

- The number of restaurants reviewed
- The number of active restaurants (that is, restaurant page owners logging in)
- The number of users
- The number of active users
- Searches performed
- Reviews placed
- Ads purchased
- The direction and rate of change for all of the above

That all looks pretty sound, though I would consider adding one more: net promoter score (NPS). Let's add two perspectives to our list:

- NPS from users
- NPS from restaurants

And that wraps up the business section. Let's move on to what we learned in Chapter 6: frontend monitoring.

Frontend Monitoring

As you might recall from Chapter 6, there is really only one big thing we need to make sure we've got: RUM metrics (use your favorite frontend monitoring tool). This will allow us to keep tabs on page load times from the user perspective.

Application and Server Monitoring

The first thing we'll need for this section is an architecture diagram of *Tater.ly*'s infrastructure (Figure 11-1):

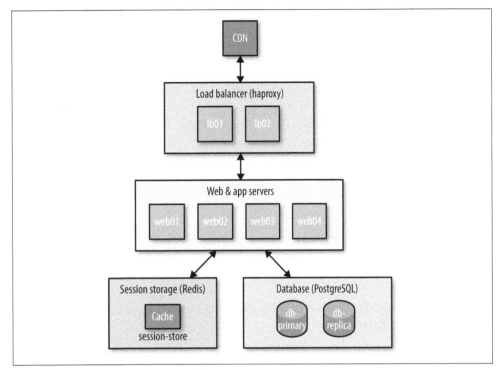

Figure 11-1. Tater.ly architecture diagram

From this architecture diagram, we can see that we have a standard three-tier architecture, plus a few other bits. Traffic comes in through a CDN with the origin set to our load balancers (2x) in an active-active configuration, 4x web servers (on which the Django app also lives), a PostgreSQL database in primary-replica configuration, and a single Redis server for session storage. *Tater.ly* uses a web hosting provider rather than their own datacenters, so managing hardware and network is of low concern to them.

Drawing upon the lessons we learned in chapters 7 and 9, what metrics and logs can you spot? Here's what I've got:

Metrics:

- Page load time
- User logins: successes, failures, length of time taken, daily active users, weekly active users
- Searches: number performed, latency
- Reviews: reviews submitted, latency
- PostgreSQL (inside the app): query latency

- PostgreSQL (at the database server): transactions per second
- Redis (inside the app): query latency
- Redis (at the Redis server): transactions per second, hit/miss ratio, cache eviction rate
- CDN: hit/miss ratio, latency to origin
- haproxy: requests per second, healthy/unhealthy backends, HTTP response codes at frontend and backend
- Apache: requests per second, HTTP response codes
- Standard OS metrics: CPU utilization, memory utilization, network throughput, disk IOPS and space

Logs:

- User logins: user ID, context (success? failure? reason for failure?)
- Django: exceptions/tracebacks
- The service logs for all the server-side daemons we're using: Apache, PostgreSQL, Redis log, and haproxy

Any synthetic website monitoring tool can provide us with another crucial piece of information: SSL certificate expiration.

Security Monitoring

As *Tater.ly* isn't subject to any compliance or regulatory requirements, security monitoring is straightforward:

- SSH: login attempts and failures
- syslog logs
- auditd logs

Alerting

And lastly, we going to need some alerts. Chapter 3 taught us that we don't need a whole lot to be effective. Looking at the metrics and logs we've identified, I would expect these alerts to be in place:

- Page load time increasing
- Increasing error rates and latency on Redis, Apache, and haproxy

- Increasing error rates and/or latency for certain application actions: searches, review submissions, user logins
- Increasing latency on PostgreSQL queries

Make sure to write up a runbook or two for the application with all of this newfound information so your colleagues can benefit from all this knowledge and visibility.

Wrap-Up

And that's it! Congratulations, you just finished your first monitoring assessment—that wasn't so hard, was it? Of course, this is only the beginning of your monitoring journey. Monitoring is never *done*, since the business, application, and infrastructure will continue to evolve over time. This assessment is a great starting point, but don't forget to keep improving.

An Example Runbook: Demo App

This is an example runbook (mentioned in Chapter 3) for you to use in your own environment. This is a great starting point, and I encourage you to build on this and iterate over time. A runbook is only as good as the information in it, so if you find you need different sections, by all means, create them!

Demo App

The Rails Demo App is a simple Rails blog app, showing off how a basic Rails app might look. The main components are a database-backed user management system and a post/comment system.

Metadata

The codebase is located in the internal source code system under the name demo-app.

The service owner is John Doe.

Escalation Procedure

In the event assistance is needed to resolve an issue with this service, the service owner has requested to be the next escalation point. See the company contact sheet for contact instructions.

External Dependencies

No external dependencies

Internal Dependencies

PostgreSQL database, running on an RDS instance located at *rds-123.foo.com*.

Tech Stack

- Rails 4.x
- PostgreSQL (AWS RDS)

Metrics and Logs

The app emits the following metrics:

- User login (count)
- User logout (count)
- Post create (count)
- Post delete (count)
- Comment create (count)
- Comment delete (count)
- Post create time (timer)
- Post delete time (timer)
- User signup time (timer)
- User login time (timer)
- User logout time (timer)

The app emits the following logs:

- User signin with user ID, status (success/fail), and IP address
- Post create with user ID, status (success/fail), and IP address
- Comment create with user ID, status (success/fail), and IP address

Alerts

User signin failure rate
> This alert fires when the rate of user signin failures goes above 5% in a 5 m
> period. Potential causes are a bad deploy (check for recent deploys) or a brute
> force attack (check the user signin log for signs of an attack).

User login time too high

This alert fires when the time it takes for a user to login exceeds one second. Check for a recent bad deploy or an issue with Postgres performance.

Post create time too high

This alert fires when the time it takes for a user to create a post exceeds one second. Check for a recent bad deploy or an issue with Postgres performance.

Comment create time too high

This alert fires when the time it takes for a user to create a comment exceeds one second. Check for a recent bad deploy or an issue with Postgres performance.

Availability Chart

As mentioned in Chapter 4, Table B-1 is a chart of availability numbers. It's a great reference for how much downtime is allowed within a given availability target.

Table B-1. Availability (chart thanks to Wikipedia (https://en.wikipedia.org/wiki/High_avail ability))

Availability %	Downtime per year	Downtime per month	Downtime per week	Downtime per day
90% ("one nine")	36.5 days	72 hours	16.8 hours	2.4 hours
95% ("one and a half nines")	18.25 days	36 hours	8.4 hours	1.2 hours
97%	10.96 days	21.6 hours	5.04 hours	43.2 minutes
98%	7.30 days	14.4 hours	3.36 hours	28.8 minutes
99% ("two nines")	3.65 days	7.20 hours	1.68 hours	14.4 minutes
99.5% ("two and a half nines")	1.83 days	3.60 hours	50.4 minutes	7.2 minutes
99.8%	17.52 hours	86.23 minutes	20.16 minutes	2.88 minutes
99.9% ("three nines")	8.76 hours	43.8 minutes	10.1 minutes	1.44 minutes
99.95% ("three and a half nines")	4.38 hours	21.56 minutes	5.04 minutes	43.2 seconds
99.99% ("four nines")	52.56 minutes	4.38 minutes	1.01 minutes	8.64 seconds
99.995% ("four and a half nines")	26.28 minutes	2.16 minutes	30.24 seconds	4.32 seconds
99.999% ("five nines")	5.26 minutes	25.9 seconds	6.05 seconds	864.3 milliseconds
99.9999% ("six nines")	31.5 seconds	2.59 seconds	604.8 milliseconds	86.4 milliseconds
99.99999% ("seven nines")	3.15 seconds	262.97 milliseconds	60.48 milliseconds	8.64 milliseconds
99.999999% ("eight nines")	315.569 milliseconds	26.297 milliseconds	6.048 milliseconds	0.864 milliseconds
99.9999999% ("nine nines")	31.5569 milliseconds	2.6297 milliseconds	0.6048 milliseconds	0.0864 milliseconds

Index

systems resiliency and stability, 38

T

TCP versus UDP, 106
throughput, 116, 118
tools, 3-8
    building, 7
    buying versus building, 25-28
    cargo-culting tools, 6
    choosing, 5-7
    cost considerations, 26, 27
    mapping to dashboards, 8
    observation tools, 5
    standardization of, 6
    tool creep, 5
    tool fragmentation, 5
total addressable market (TAM), 59
traditional versus cloud architectures, 12
TSDB (time series database), 19

U

UDP versus TCP, 106

unstructured logs, 18-19, 84
user perspective in monitoring, 24, 57

V

visualization of data, 20-21
voice and video performance, 119

W

web server performance, 98-100
WebpageTest.org, 67, 71, 72
weekly active users (WAU), 59
whitebox monitoring, 67

Y

Yelp, 60-61

Z

zone transfers, 102

About the Author

Mike Julian is a consultant who helps companies build better monitoring for their applications and infrastructure. He is the Editor of *Monitoring Weekly*, an online publication about all-things-monitoring. Mike has previously worked as an operations/DevOps engineer for Taos Consulting, Peak Hosting, Oak Ridge National Lab, and others.

Mike is from Knoxville, Tennessee, and lives in San Francisco, California. Outside of work, he spends his time driving mountain roads in a classic BMW, reading, and traveling.

You find find Mike at:

- *https://www.mikejulian.com*
- *Aster Labs (https://www.AsterLabs.io)*
- *Monitoring Weekly (https://weekly.monitoring.love)*

Colophon

The animal on the cover of *Practical Monitoring*, the Bengal monitor (*Varanus bengalensis*), is a diurnal monitor lizard found across southern and western Asia. Dwelling primarily in low-elevation areas, they are adaptable enough to survive in a variety of habitats with varying degrees of moisture and vegetation, from forests, to bogs, to agricultural zones. They are known to grow to a length of 175 cm (100 cm of which comprise the tail), and have few predators in adulthood, aside from humans, who hunt monitors for their meat and fat, as well as their skin, which is used as the drum head for the kanjira, a hand-percussion instrument.

Though subsisting primarily on arthropods, Bengal monitors are known to eat most creatures small enough to overpower, including a wide variety of vertebrates, birds, and fish, as well as occasional fruits and vegetables. The Bengal mating season lasts from June through September, and female monitors bury their clutch of eggs, taking care to compact the soil over the nest while digging poorly-concealed decoy nests in the surrounding area.

Monitor lizards have a higher metabolism than most reptiles and spend most of their waking moments engaged in eating and physical activity. They are strong swimmers, capable of high speeds on the ground, in the water, and while scaling trees, where they take the eggs from birds' nests and consume sleeping bats.

Many of the animals on O'Reilly covers are endangered; all of them are important to the world. To learn more about how you can help, go to *animals.oreilly.com*.

The cover image is from John George Wood's *Animate Creation*. The cover fonts are URW Typewriter and Guardian Sans. The text font is Adobe Minion Pro; the heading font is Adobe Myriad Condensed; and the code font is Dalton Maag's Ubuntu Mono.

Learn from experts.
Find the answers you need.

Sign up for a **10-day free trial** to get **unlimited access** to all of the content on Safari, including Learning Paths, interactive tutorials, and curated playlists that draw from thousands of ebooks and training videos on a wide range of topics, including data, design, DevOps, management, business—and much more.

Start your free trial at:

oreilly.com/safari

(No credit card required)

Milton Keynes UK
Ingram Content Group UK Ltd.
UKHW030759190724
445759UK00003B/6